Zacharias Tanee Fomum

THE MINISTRY OF SUPPLICATION

(THE BARRENNESS, AWAKENING, BATTLE AND TRIUMPH OF HANNAH)

Éditions du Livre Chrétien
4, rue du Révérend Père Cloarec
92400 Courbevoie France
editionlivrechretien@gmail.com

© Zacharias Tanee Fomum, 1997
ALL RIGHTS RESERVED

Printed by :
Editions du livre chrétien
4, rue du Révérend Père Cloarec
92400 Courbevoie - FRANCE
Tél : (33) 9 52 29 27 72
Email : editionlivrechretien@gmail.com

Cover :
Jacques Maré

I lovingly dedicate this book to
EMILIA AKWONG TENDO
a lover of Lord Jesus Christ,
a prayer woman,
my friend and fellow woker
with gratitude and in glorious expectation.

TABLE OF CONTENTS

    Preface 9

1. The Barrenness, Awakening, Battle and Triumph of Hannah...11

2. Prayer...15

3. Prayerlessness..27

4. Spiritual Genetics 31

5. Spiritual Barrenness 39

6. And Prayer...39

7. The Physical Barrenness Of Hannah 59

8. The Ministry Of Provocation 67

9. The Battle To Give God A Prophet For Israel :
   A Vision Of God's Burden 77

10. The Battle To Give God A Prophet For Israel :
    The Separation Of Hannah From The Others.............................83

11. The Battle To Give God A Prophet For Israel :
    The Bitterness Of Soul Of Hannah..87

12. The Battle To Give God A Prophet For Israel :
    The Much Weeping Of Hannah...93

13. The Battle To Give God A Prophet For Israel :
    The Fasting Of Hannah..103

14. The Battle To Give God A Prophet For Israel :
    Hannah Prayed To The Lord 111

15. The Battle To Give God A Prophet For Israel :
    Hannah's Request 117

16. The Battle To Give God A Prophet For Israel :
    Hannah's Supplication Through A Vow 129

17. The Battle To Give God A Prophet For Israel :
    Hannah's Importunity 151

18. The Battle To Give God A Prophet For Israel :
    Hannah Praying In The Heart 157

19. The Battle to Give God a Prophet for Israel :
    Hannah Misunderstood 163

20. The Battle To Give God A Prophet For Israel :
    Hannah's Travailing Through To Victory 167

21. The Battle To Give God A Prophet For Israel :
    Hannah's Supplication And Faith 173

22. Consolidating The Gains From Supplication :
    Fulfilment Of The Vow 185

23. Consolidating The Gains From Supplication :
    Hannah's Praise And Thanksgiving 193

24. In Conclusion : A Praying Prophet 199

PREFACE

This book, "**THE MINISTRY OF SUPPLICATION**", is the tenth book in the Prayer Series. The books in this series that have already been written are :

1. The Way of Victorious Praying
2. The Ministry of Fasting
3. The Art of Intercession
4. The Practice of Intercession
5. Prayer With Power
6. Moving God Through Prayer
7. Practical Spiritual Warfare Through Prayer
8. The Ministry of Praise and Thanksgiving
9. Waiting on the Lord in Prayer
10. **The Ministry of Supplication**

God answers prayers. If people are desperate enough to seek His will, know what He wants and then wrestle to see it come to reality, it will become a reality. Hannah had a problem. Her problem was a kind of national problem because the nation desperately needed a prophet, and her first son had to occupy that post and function in that office. Initially, she was complacent in her barrenness, but the ministry of provocation, which she received from Peninnah, stirred her to wrestle with tears, fasting, vowing, more tears, bitterness of soul, anguish of soul, great anguish and great grief, until she moved God to hear her and answer her.

In moving God to provide her need, she also moved God to provide the need of His people.

May the Lord mightily touch you as you read this book! May it move you to abandon all that must be abandoned in order that you may be abundantly fruitful! May your eyes be opened to your potential to execute God's will by seeing His cause, making His cause your cause and asking Him to move through your supplication to make an individual, a family, a town, a nation, nations and continents of the earth your possession for Him!

Glory be to His Name in the highest!

> Zacharias Tanee Fomum,
> P.O.Box 6090,
> Yaounde,
> Cameroon.
> 22nd September 1997.

CHAPTER 1

THE BARRENNESS, AWAKENING, BATTLE AND TRIUMPH OF HANNAH

"There was a certain man from Ramathaim, a Zuphite from the hill country of Ephraim, whose name was Elkanah son of Jeroham, the son of Elihu, the son of Tohu, the son of Zuph, an Ephraimite. He had two wives; one was called Hannah and the other Peninnah. Peninnah had children, but Hannah had none.

Year after year this man went up from his town to worship and sacrifice to the Lord Almighty at Shiloh, where Hophni and Phinehas, the two sons of Eli, were priests of the Lord. Whenever the day came for Elkanah to sacrifice, he would give portions of the meat to his wife Peninnah and to all her sons and daughters. But to Hannah he gave a double portion because he loved her, and the Lord had closed her womb. And because the Lord had closed her womb, her rival kept provoking her in order to irritate her. This went on year after year. Whenever Hannah went up to the house of the Lord, her rival provoked her till she wept and would not eat. Elkanah her husband would say to her, 'Hannah, why are you weeping? Why don't you eat? Why are you downhearted? Don't I mean more to you than ten sons?'

Once when they had finished eating and drinking in Shiloh, Hannah stood up. Now Eli the priest was sitting on a chair by the doorpost of the Lord's temple. In bitterness of soul Hannah wept much and prayed to the Lord. And she made a vow, saying, 'O Lord Almighty, if you will only look upon your servant's misery and remember me, and not forget your servant but give her a son, then I will give him to the Lord for all the days of his life, and no razor will ever be used on his head.'

As she kept on praying to the Lord, Eli observed her mouth. Hannah was praying in her heart, and her lips were moving but her voice was not heard. Eli thought she was drunk and said to her, 'How long will you keep on getting drunk? Get rid of your wine.'

'Not so, my lord,' Hannah replied, 'I am a woman who is deeply troubled. I have not been drinking wine or beer; I was pouring out my soul to the Lord. Do not take your servant for a wicked woman; I have been

praying here out of my great anguish and grief.'

Eli answered, 'Go in peace, and may the God of Israel grant you what you have asked of him.'

She said, 'May your servant find favour in your eyes.' Then she went her way and ate something, and her face was no longer downcast.

Early the next morning they arose and worshipped before the Lord and then went back to their home at Ramah. Elkanah lay with Hannah his wife, and the Lord remembered her. So in the course of time Hannah conceived and gave birth to a son. She named him Samuel, saying, 'Because I asked the Lord for him.'

When the man Elkanah went up with all his family to offer the annual sacrifice to the Lord and to fulfil his vow, Hannah did not go. She said to her husband, 'After the boy is weaned, I will take him and present him before the Lord, and he will live there always.'

'Do what seems best to you,' Elkanah her husband told her. 'Stay here until you have weaned him; only may the Lord make good his word.' So the woman stayed at home and nursed her son until she had weaned him.

After he was weaned, she took the boy with her, young as he was, along with a three-year-old bull, an ephah of flour and a skin of wine, and brought him to the house of the Lord at Shiloh.
When they had slaughtered the bull, they brought the boy to Eli, and she said to him, 'As surely as you live, my lord, I am the woman who stood here beside you praying to the Lord. I prayed for this child, and the Lord has granted me what I asked of him. So now I give him to the Lord. For his whole life he will be given over to the Lord.' And he worshipped the Lord there" (1 Samuel 1 : 1-28).

Then Hannah prayed and said: *"My heart rejoices in the Lord; in the Lord my horn is lifted high. My mouth boasts over my enemies, for I delight in your deliverance. There is no-one holy like the Lord; there is no-one besides you; there is no Rock like our God. Do not keep talking so proudly or let your mouth speak such arrogance, for the Lord is a God who knows, and by him deeds are weighed. The bows of the warriors are broken, but those who stumbled are armed with strength. Those who were full hire themselves out for food, but those who were hungry hunger no more. She who was barren has borne seven children, but she who has had many sons pines away. The Lord brings death and makes alive; he brings down to the grave and raises up. The Lord sends poverty and wealth; he humbles and he exalts. He raises the poor from the dust and lifts the needy from the ash heap; he seats them with princes and has them inherit a throne of honour. For the foundations of the earth are the Lord's; upon them he has set the world. He will guard the feet of his saints, but the wicked will be silenced in darkness. It is not by strength that one prevails; those who oppose the Lord will be shattered. He will thunder against them from heaven; the Lord will judge the ends of the earth. He will give strength to his king and exalt the horn of his anointed"* (1 Samuel 2:1-10).

CHAPTER 2

PRAYER

1. One must settle down in the Lord's presence before one can touch the Throne. It is in the stillness of the Holiest that the Father speaks. It is when we are quiet that the Holy Spirit prays through us. In order to have such definite prayer meetings for revival, Christians must be willing to sacrifice social pleasantries, and the comforts of life, including even sleep, and to lay aside everything that would hinder them in having these trysts with God (James A. Steward).

2. No one can become a real praying soul unless intense application is the price. I am convinced the difference between the saints like Wesley, Fletcher, Brainerd, Bramwell, Bounds and ourselves is energy, perseverance - invincible determination to prevail with God or die in the attempt.

3. Prayer is the calling upon God to do that which man cannot do on his own. What man can go ahead and do without dependence on God manifested through prayer is of no consequence. It is the fruit of man's will, thoughts and feelings and, because these are all flesh, it is obvious that prayerlessness leads to the work of the flesh.

4. Prayerless preaching, prayerless giving, prayerless serving are all activities of the flesh. They produce the products that God labels wood, hay, stubble.

5. It requires faith to pray. It requires more faith to fast and pray. To seek the Lord in fasting-prayer shows greater desire, greater determination and greater faith. Our prayers for revival without fasting are too often shallow and insincere. Fasting is potent proof to God that we are willing to pay the price in sincerity, in fervour, in single-heartedness in our prayers for His rulings and

overrulings, in the affairs of this and every nation.. (Sarah Foulkes Moore).

6. Prayer was one of the fundamentally important facets of early church life. It was the church in prayer that guaranteed a church of power. It was prayer that kept them in touch with their ascended Lord, it was prayer that enabled miracles to happen in the lives of the individuals (Brian Mills).

7. The early church was formed in prayer, continued praying, and grew in size and depth as it prayed. There was such power generated when they prayed that God answered prayer whenever they met together (Brian Mills).

8. The more men pray, the less worldly they become. The less they pray, the more worldly they become (Leonard Ravenhill).

9. The life of distinctively christian praying must be built upon solid foundations. Spasmodic , intermittent, situational praying in times of crisis may be able to rest on the immediate occasion and need. But stable and sustained praying will need to rest on something much more solid and enduring. Praying primarily based upon the felt need of the moment will be a very different kind of praying from that which is rooted and grounded in deep truths concerning both God and man (Charles Whiston).

10. Prayer may be either self-centred or God-centred, and these are two very different kinds of praying.

11. Let us seek to lay a firm, deep, Biblical base upon which christian praying may be built. Let us begin by turning away from

ourselves to Jesus Christ, the Man of prayer. He will teach us to pray and He will lead us into prayer and grant us to succeed in praying.

12. Ask for what you need now and, as a rule, keep to present needs; ask for your daily bread — what you want now — ask for that. Ask for it plainly, as before God, Who does not regard your fine expressions, and to Whom your eloquence and oratory will be less than nothing and vanity. Thou art before the Lord ; let thy words be few, but let thy heart be fervent (Charles H. Spurgeon).

13. There should be a looking round the blessing which you desire to see if it is assuredly a fitting thing to ask; for some prayers would never be offered if men did but think. A little reflection would show us that some things which we desire were better left alone. We may, moreover, have a motive at the bottom of our desire which is not Christ-like, a selfish motive, which forgets God's glory and caters only for our own ease and comfort. Although we may ask for things which are for our profit, yet still we must never let our profit interfere in any way with the glory of God (Charles H. Spurgeon).

14. Prayer is an act which only the Holy Spirit can teach us. He is the Giver of all prayer. Pray for prayer — pray till you can pray ; pray to be helped to pray, and give not up praying because thou canst not pray, for it is when thou thinkest thou cannot pray that thou art most praying (Charles H. Spurgeon).

15. The best prayers I have ever heard in our prayer meetings have been those which have been full of arguments. Sometimes my soul has been fairly melted down when I have listened to brethren who have come before God feeling the mercy seat was

really needed, and that they must have it; for they first pleaded with God to give it for this reason, and then for a second, and then for a third, and then for a fourth and a fifth, until they have awakened the fervency of the entire assembly (Charles H. Spurgeon).

16. If God's mercies came to us unasked, they would not be half so useful as they are now, when they have to be sought for ; for now we get a double blessing, a blessing in the obtaining, and a blessing in the seeking. The very act of prayer is a blessing. To pray is as if it were to bathe oneself in a cool purling stream, and so to escape from the heat of earth's summer sun. To pray is to mount on eagle's wings above the clouds and get into the clear heaven where God dwelleth. To pray is to enter the treasure-house of God and to enrich oneself out of an inexhaustible storehouse. To pray is to grasp heaven in one's arms, to embrace the Deity within one's soul, and to feed one's body that has been made a temple of the Holy Spirit. Apart from the answer, prayer is itself a benediction. To pray, my brethren, is to cast off your burdens, it is to tear away your rags, it is to shake off your diseases, it is to be filled with spiritual vigour, it is to reach the highest point of christian health. (Charles H. Spurgeon, "12 Sermons on Prayer" Maranatha Publications, Benin City, Nigeria).

17. True prayer is an approach of the soul by the Spirit of God to the throne of God (Spurgeon).

18. God rules the world just as He rules the church by prayer (E.M. Bounds).

19. Nothing is more important to God than prayer in dealing with mankind. But it is likewise all-important to man to pray (E.M.

Bounds).

20. Man must pray to God if love for God is to exist. Faith, hope and patience, and all the strong, beautiful, vital forces of piety are withered and dead in a prayerless life. The life of the individual believer, his personal salvation, and personal christian graces have their being, bloom and fruitage in prayer (E.M. Bounds).

21. Prayer concerns God, whose purposes and plans are conditioned on prayer. His will and His glory are bound up in prayer. The days of God's splendour and renown have always been great days of prayer. God's great movements in this world have been conditioned on, continued and fashioned by prayer. God has put Himself in these great movements just as men have prayed. Present, prevailing, conspicuous and mastering prayer has always brought God to be present (E.M. Bounds).

22. The real and obvious test of a genuine work of God is the prevalence of the spirit of prayer (E.M. Bounds).

23. God's mightiest forces surcharge and impregnate a movement when prayer's mightiest forces are there (E.M. Bounds).

24. The prayers of God's saints are a great factor, a supreme factor, in carrying forward God's work, with facility and in time. When the church is in the condition of prayer, God's cause always flourishes and His kingdom on earth always triumphs.

25. It is according to the divine plans that spiritual prosperity comes through the prayer channel. Praying saints are God's agents for

carrying on His saving and providential work on earth. If His agents fail Him, neglecting to pray, then His work fails. Praying agents of the Most High are always forerunners of spiritual prosperity (E.M. Bounds).

26. The life, the vigour, the motive-power of God's work is formed by praying men. The men to whom Jesus Christ committed the fortunes and destiny of His church were men of prayer. To no other kind of men has God ever committed Himself in this world. The apostles were pre-eminently men of prayer. They gave themselves to prayer. They made praying their chief business. It was first in point of importance and it was first in results. God never has and He never will commit the weighty interests of His kingdom to prayerless men, who do not make prayer a conspicuous and controlling factor in their lives. Men who do not pray never rise to any eminence of piety. Men of piety are always men of prayer. Men who are not pre-eminently men of prayer are never noted for the simplicity and strength of their faith. Piety flourishes nowhere so rapidly and so rankly as in the closet. The closet is the garden of faith (E.M. Bounds, "The Weapon of Prayer" Baker Book House, Grand Rapids, Michigan 49516, USA).

27. Prayer is partnership with God in His planet-sized purposes (Herald Newsletter).

28. Praying is fighting, spirit-fighting. That is to say, the Apostle Paul says we are in the thick of a fight. There is a war on. How shall we best fight? First get into good shape to pray, and then with all your praying strength and skill, pray. This is the sort of action that turns the enemy's flank, and reveals his heels. He simply cannot stand before persistent knee-work (Herald Newsletter).

29. Prayer concerns three, not two but three : God to whom we pray, the man on the contested earth who prays, and the evil one against whom we pray. And the purpose of the prayer is not to persuade or influence God, but to join forces with Him against the enemy. Not towards God, but with God against Satan.... that is the main thing to keep in mind in prayer. The real pitch is not Godward but Satanward (Herald Newsletter).

30. The second intense truth is this : the winning quality in prayer is persistence. The final test is here. This is the last ditch. Many who fight well up to this point lose their grip here, and so lose all. Many who are well equipped for prayer fail here, and doubtless fail because they have not rightly understood. With clear, ringing tones the Master's voice sounds in our hearts again today, "always to pray, and not to faint" (Herald Newsletter).

31. The great essential, Jesus says, is prayer.... The great essential in prayer is persistence. The temptation in prayer is that one may lose heart, and give up, or give in (Herald Newsletter).

32. Satan believes in the potency of prayer. He fears it. He can hinder its results for a while. He does his best to hinder it, and to hinder it as long as possible (Herald Newsletter).

33. Prayer overcomes Satan. It defeats his plans and himself. He cannot successfully stand before it. He trembles when some man of simple faith in God prays. Prayer is insistence upon God's will being done. It needs for its practice a man in sympathetic touch with God. Its basis is Jesus' victory. It overcomes the opposing will of the great traitor-leader (Herald Newsletter).

34. A true champion is nourished on time sp_ prayer. He gets his sustenance for the day, n_ table, but in the prayer closet. Prayer is more imp_ than food when it comes to energy for serving God, a_ he can go forth to do some great work for the Lord, he _ first retreat to Him in prayer (Lester Sumrall).

35. The litmus test of any person's spiritual character is his prayer life. Real success comes not from the work we do when the world is watching, but from the life we live when no one can see. No man or woman who fails at prayer can be truly successful at any endeavour for God. Regardless of what your gift is, no matter what God has called you to do, the secret to ultimate victory is the victory you gain in secret. The most important aspect of your calling is your prayer life (Lester Sumrall).

36. We are all called to pray (Lester Sumrall).

37. Prayer is not for God's benefit but for ours. We are commanded to pray, not because God needs information or the attention, but because we need the experience of knowing and demonstrating that we depend on Him (Lester Sumrall).

38. God is glorified when He can respond specifically to our prayers (Lester Sumrall).

39. A man of prayer is always a man of vision. The more he prays, the more intimately he knows God. The more intimately he knows God, the more able he is to see things with a divine perspective. And a man who sees things with a divine perspective is a man of great vision (Lester Sumrall).

Prayer is the place where our greatest battles must be won (Lester Sumrall).

41. Prayer does indeed change things. It changes us. It strengthens our faith. It helps us to see things through God's eyes. It softens our hearts. It sensitizes our consciences. It gives us supernatural courage (Lester Sumrall, " The Making of a Champion " Thomas Nelson Publishers, Nashville, Tennessee, USA).

42. Prayer is a means of communication that we have with God, a manner of life that should characterize our living, and a ministry that God has entrusted to us for others. Personal praying is a denial of our independence - we are looking to God and saying that we must trust Him. Corporate prayer is a recognition of our inter-dependence — we are sharing with each other and articulating common longings as we come to God (Brian Mills).

43. Prayer is enriching, too. It's us as creatures being in touch with the Creator. It is man and God working together. It's the subject and the King, it's the servant and the Master ; it's the student and the Teacher ; it's the child and the Father ; it's the human and the Divine co-operating together, sharing together, living together, working together, talking with each other, causing the plans of heaven to be worked out on earth, and the concerns of earth to be represented in heaven (Brian Mills, " Prayer Triplets " Anzea Publishers, Australia).

44. Prayer does business with God. Prayer creates hunger for souls ; hunger for souls creates prayer. The understanding soul prays ; the praying soul gets understanding. To the soul who prays in self-owed weakness, the Lord gives His strength. Oh that we

were men of prayer like Elijah, a man subject to like passions as we are! Lord, let us pray. Prayer is the simplest form of speech that infant lips can try , and yet so sublime that it outranges all speech and exhausts man's vocabulary (Leonard Ravenhill), " Why Revival Tarries " Bethany Fellowship Publishers, Minneapolis, USA).

45. The way to pray is by starting to pray.

46. Start to pray today.

47. Set an hour for prayer daily.

48. Make sure that hour is used for prayer.

49. Continue to pray for that one hour for one month.

50. Continue for a second month.

51. Increase the one hour to one hour and a half.

52. Go on that way.

53. You are making progress.

54. God bless you ! Amen.

CHAPTER 3

Prayerlessness

1. Failure to pray is failure along the whole line of life (E.M. Bounds).

2. Failure to pray is failure of duty, failure of service, and failure in spiritual progress. God must help man by prayer. He who does not pray, therefore, robs himself of God's help and places God where He cannot help man (E.M. Bounds).

3. When the church fails to pray, God's cause decays and evil of every kind prevails. In other words, God works through the prayers of His people, and when they fail Him at this point, decline and deadness ensue (E.M. Bounds).

4. God's secrets, councils, and cause have never been committed to prayerless men. Neglect of prayer has always brought loss of faith, loss of love, and loss of prayer. Failure to pray has been the baneful, inevitable cause of backsliding and estrangement from God (E.M. Bounds).

5. Prayerless men have stood in the way of God fulfilling His Word and doing His will on earth. They tie the divine hands and interfere with God in His gracious designs. As praying men are a help to God, so prayerless men are a hindrance to Him (E.M. Bounds).

6. The Holy Spirit never descends upon prayerless men. He never fills them. He never empowers them. There is nothing whatever in common between the Spirit of God and men who do no pray (E.M. Bounds).

7. Prayerless men misrepresent God in all His work and in all His plans (E.M. Bounds) .

8. God's purposes are being delayed ; delayed because of our unwillingness to learn how to pray or our slowness of learning (Herald Newsletter).

9. The real reason for the delay or failure lies simply in the difference between God's view-point and ours. In our asking either we have not reached the wisdom that asks best or we have not reached the unselfishness that is willing to sacrifice a good thing for a better or the best, the unselfishness that is willing to sacrifice the smaller personal desire for the larger thing that affects the lives of many (Herald Newsletter).

10. Satan has the power to hold back the answer for a while ; to delay the results for a time. He has not the power to hold it back finally if someone understands and prays with quiet, steady, persistence. The real pitch of prayer therefore is Satanward...(Herald Newsletter) .

11. God won't use a man who loves to put himself on a pedestal before men ; He chooses instead those who spend time on their knees before the throne of grace (Lester Sumrall).

12. If we lose the battle in prayer, we have lost the battle completely (Lester Sumrall).

CHAPTER 4

SPIRITUAL GENETICS

> "*There was a certain man from Ramathaim, a Zuphite from the hill country of Ephraim, whose name was Elkanah son of Jeroham, the son of Elihu, the son of Tohu, the son of zuph, an Ephraimite*" (1Samuel 1 :1).

The Bible could simply have said, "There was a certain man from Ramathaim, a Zuphite from the hill country of Ephraim, whose name was Elkanah." However, the Bible adds that Elkanah was the son of Jeroham. It further adds that Jeroham was the son of Elihu. It continues that Elihu was the son of Tohu and that Tohu was the son of Zuph. We know that the Holy Spirit had a reason for causing this Scripture to be presented this way. We can put it out as follows :

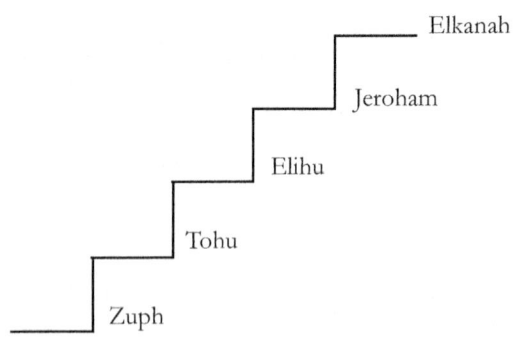

We say without hesitation that what Zuph was, was in some measure found in Elkanah. Elkanah was already in Zuph and, to some extent, Elkanah did what Zuph did, and Elkanah learnt and imbibed what was in Zuph and what Zuph did. The spiritual content of Zuph was reflected in some measure in Elkanah. This also means that what Elkanah was, influenced his descendants in many generations to come. We can put it this way:

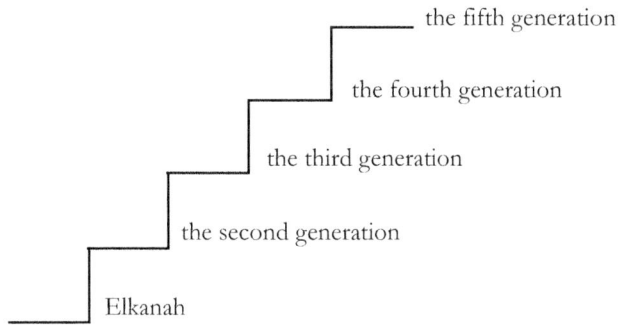

What we are saying can be seen in the following :

Max Jules, the atheist, lived a godless life. He married an ungodly girl. From that union the following were produced :
- 310 who were paupers,
- 150 were criminals,
- 7 were murderers,
- 100 were drunkards,
- more than half of the women were prostitutes.

His 540 known descendants cost the United States government 1.250.000 dollars.

Jonathan Edwards, the revivalist, lived at the same time as the atheist Max Jules. He married a godly girl. An investigation was made of his 1,394 known descendants. The investigation revealed the following about them :
- 13 became university presidents (vice-chancellors, rectors),
- 65 became university teachers,
- 3 became United States Senators,
- 30 became judges,
- 100 became lawyers,

- 60 became medical doctors,
- 75 became army and navy officials,
- 100 became preachers and missionaries,
- 60 became authors of prominence,
- 1 became a Vice-President of the United States of America,
- 80 became public officers in other capacities,
- 295 became university graduates among whom were the following :
  - state governors,
  - diplomats,
  - and so on.

None of his descendants cost the United States government a dime. (Quoted From The Book, " Meat for Men " by Leonard Ravenhill, Bethany Fellowship Publishers, Minneapolis).

It is obvious that spiritual genetics is real. It is foolish to ignore it. The Lord God put the same matter in other words by saying, *"The Lord, the Lord, the compassionate and gracious God, slow to anger, abounding in love and faithfulness, maintaining love to thousands, and forgiving wickedness, rebellion and sin. Yet he does not leave the guilty unpunished ; he punishes the children and their children for the sin of the fathers to the third and fourth generation"* (Exodus 34 :6-7). Again the Bible says, *" I, the Lord your God, am a jealous God, punishing the children for the sin of the fathers to the third and fourth generation of those who hate me, but showing love to a thousand generations of those who love me and keep my commandments "* (Exodus 20 :5-6).

SPIRITUAL GENETICS AND PRAYER

The man or woman of prayer will beget children who are men and women of prayer. The man or woman who does not pray will give birth to children who are unlikely to be people of prayer.

The Lord has called all who are His to the primary task of prayer. Those who heed His call and obey will satisfy God's heart and lay a foundation for their children who will follow suit. Those who ignore the Lord's invitation to pray will also lay a foundation for their children - a foundation of prayerlessness. Do you love your children ? If you do, become a man or woman of prayer; so that they too will become men and women of prayer. Please do something about it. Why not break the habit of sleeping until six o'clock in the morning and begin to wake up at five o'clock in the morning to pray ? Why not make progress and begin to give yourself two hours of prayer each morning by waking up at four o'clock ? You will of course sacrifice sleep, but you will gain in a more intimate relationship with God and in more influence on your circumstances and the people of God, as well as the world at large. Prayer is the determining factor, and the person who prays determines what happens to those for whom he prays.

If you give yourself two hours of prayer everyday, you will be praying for 730 hours a year. It means that in twenty years you will have prayed for 14600 hours. This means that you will have prayed for more than one and a half years ! If these 14600 hours of prayer are well invested, they could contribute to a major spiritual revolution ! On the other hand, if you give that time to sleep, in twenty years you will realize that you gained nothing by sleeping.

Another aspect of spiritual genetics is that the local church to which you belong will influence your prayer life and prepare you to impart to the coming spiritual generation what you have received. You should think about this seriously. If I were in a situation in which I had to choose what church to belong to, one of the determinant factors would be the prayer life of the church. The churches that have a fixed lengthening period set aside for prayer is serious. If all or most of the members of that church gather at the time set aside to pray and actually pray, God will move and things will be different. For your own good and for the good of your physical and spiritual children, make sure that you are a member of a church that prays seriously. If the praying is serious, two things will be obvious - there will be growth in Christ-likeness and growth in numbers !

BE A STARTING POINT

You may discover that neither your father nor your mother prayed seriously. You may find that the genes in you do not carry an inclination to pray. What should you do then ? Should you blame yourself and give up ? The answer is 'No' ! God always has starting points. He started with Abraham and made him the father of faith. He can start with you. Yield yourself completely to God and begin to pray. You can start by praying for 15 minutes everyday for each day of this month. Be consistent. Make sure that there is no day during the entire month during which you do not pray for 15 minutes. Record your prayer time accurately. Mark the time at which you are starting to pray. It man be say 5.10am. Pray. When you think that you have finished praying, look at your watch. If it reads 5.25am, you can stop praying. If, on the other hand, it reads 5.20am, you should continue to pray for another five minutes. Resolve that you will not pray for less than 15 minutes everyday. Keep to this minimum by every method of self discipline possible. Remember that the world belongs to the disciplined of this world. The Kingdom of God is also a possession of believers who discipline themselves.

Having gained the grounds of praying for at least 15 minutes everyday, you can now move on to praying for 20 minutes a day during the coming month. Follow the same procedure as for the 15 minutes. Go on this way until the grounds of praying for 20 minutes each day are gained. Your progress can then follow the following pattern :

1st month	15 minutes
2nd month	20 minutes
3rd month	25 minutes
4th month	30 minutes
5th month	35 minutes
6th month	40 minutes
7th month	45 minutes
8th month	50 minutes
9th month	55 minutes
10th month	60 minutes

If you can faithfully pray for one hour each day, and if you do this with unchanging regularity, you will be on your way to knowing God and serving Him in a consequential way.

As you can see, someone might even begin with praying for five minutes everyday in January and then move on to ten minutes of prayer in February. He can then move to 15 minutes in March and by December, he will be praying for one hour each day.

The question may arise as to how to use the time set aside for prayer. I consider that one minute periods are good and sufficient to bear one issue before God. In the first month, I will lift five things to the Lord in prayer - one per minute. I may continue to lift the same things every morning or I may ask different things each morning. Then during the second month I can set ten things aside for prayer each day. The third month with, say, fifteen minutes for prayer means that fifteen issues can be prayed about. In each case time should be taken before the time of prayer to sort out clearly what one wants to pray about. The issues to be prayed about should be written down and then prayed about systematically. Do not wait to feel or have special sensations before you pray. God answers prayers and is not guided by the emotions of the one who asks.

I expect that someone who is born again in January will be taught to pray systematically so that at the end of the year, that one will be praying for one hour everyday. Such a normal believer in prayer is likely to make much progress !

CHAPTER 5

SPIRITUAL BARRENNESS AND PRAYER

SPIRITUAL BARRENNES

1. Spiritual barrenness is the state in which a believer produces no spiritual fruit.

2. *"I am the true vine, and my Father is the gardener. He cuts off every branch in me that bears no fruit"* (John 15 :1-2).

3. *"Remain in me, and I will remain in you. No branch can bear fruit by itself ; it must remain in the vine. Neither can you bear fruit unless you remain in me"* (John 15 :4)

4. *"I am the vine ; you are the branches. If a man remains in me and I in him, he will bear much fruit ; apart from me you can do nothing"* (John 15 :5).

5. *"If anyone does not remain in me, he is like a branch that is thrown away and withers ; such branches are picked up, thrown into the fire and burned"* (John 15 :6).

6. *"If you remain in me and my words remain in you, ask whatever you wish, and it will be given you"* (John 15 :7).

7. *"This is to my Father's glory, that you bear much fruit, showing yourselves to be my disciples"* (John 15 :8).

8. *"You did not choose me, but I chose you and appointed you to go and bear fruit — fruit that will last. Then the Father will give you whatever you ask in my name"* (John 15 :16).

9. Then he told this parable : *"A man had a fig-tree, planted in his vineyard, and he went to look for fruit on it, but did not find any. So*

SPIRITUAL BARRENNESS AND PRAYER   41

he said to the man who took care of the vineyard, 'For three years now I've been coming to look for fruit on this fig-tree and I haven't found any. Cut it down ! Why should it use up the soil ?' 'Sir,' the man replied, 'leave it alone for one more year, and I'll dig round it and fertilize it. If it bears fruit next year, fine ! If not, then cut it down'" (Luke 13 : 6-8).

10. *"Listen ! A farmer went out to sow his seed. As he was scattering the seed, some fell along the path, and the birds came and ate it up. Some fell on rocky places where it did not have much soil. It sprang up quickly, because the soil was shallow. But when the sun came up, the plants were scorched, and they withered because they had no root. Other seed fell among thorns, which grew up and choked the plants, so that they did not bear grain. Still other seed fell on good soil. It came up, grew and produced a crop, multiplying thirty, sixty, or even a hundred times"* (Mark 4 : 4-8).

11. *"The farmer sows the word. Some people are like seed along the path, where the word is sown . As soon as they hear it, Satan comes and takes away the word that was sown in them. Others, like seed sown on rocky places, hear the word and at once receive it with joy. But since they have no root, they last only a short time. When trouble or persecution comes because of the word, they quickly fall away. Still others, like seed sown among thorns, hear the word ; but the worries of this life, the deceitfulness of wealth and the desires for other things come in and choke the word, making it unfruitful. Others, like seed sown on good soil, hear the word, accept it, and produce a crop - thirty, sixty or even a hundred times what was sown"* (Mark 4 :14-20).

12. *"The seed that fell among thorns stands for those who hear, but as they go on their way they are choked by life's worries, riches and pleasures, and they do not mature"* (Luke 8 :14).

13. *"Early in the morning, as he was on his way back to the city, he was*

hungry. Seeing a fig-tree by the road, he went up to it but found nothing on it except leaves. Then he said to it, 'May you never bear fruit again !' Immediately the tree withered" (Matthew 21 :18-19).

14. *"I tell you the truth, unless a grain of wheat falls to the ground and dies, it remains only a single seed. But if it dies, it produces many seeds "* (John 12 :24).

15. *"A man planted a vineyard, rented it to some farmers and went away for a long time. At harvest time he sent a servant to the tenants so they would give him some of the fruit of the vineyard. But the tenants beat him and sent him away empty-handed. He sent another servant, but that one also they beat and treated shamefully and sent away empty-handed. He sent still a third, and they wounded him and threw him out. Then the owner of the vineyard said, 'What shall I do ? I will send my son, whom I love; perhaps they will respect him.' But when the tenants saw him they talked the matter over. 'This is the heir,' they said. 'Let's kill him and the inheritance will be ours.' So they threw him out of the vineyard and killed him"* (Luke 20 :9-16).

16. He said, *"A man of noble birth went to a distant country to have himself appointed king and then to return. So he called ten of his servants and gave them ten minas. 'Put this money to work,' he said, 'until I come back.' But his subjects hated him and sent a delegation after him to say, 'We don't want this man to be our king.' He was made king , however, and returned home : Then he sent for the servants to whom he had given the money, in order to find out what they had gained with it. The first one came and said, 'Sir, your mina has earned ten more.....' The second came and said, 'Sir, your mina has earned five more.' Then another servant came and said, 'Sir, here is your mina ; I have kept it laid away in a piece of cloth. I was afraid of you, because you are a hard man. You take out what you did not put in and reap what you did not sow.' His master replied, 'I will judge you by your own words, you wicked servant ! You knew, did you, that*

I am a hard man, taking out what I did not put in, and reaping what I did not sow ? Why then didn't you put my money on deposit, so that when I came back , I could have collected it with interest ? '" (Luke 19 :12-23).

17. "*The acts of the sinful nature are obvious : sexual immorality, impurity and debauchery ; idolatry and witchcraft ; hatred, discord, jealousy, fits of rage, selfish ambition, dissension, factions and envy ; drunkenness, orgies and the like*" (Galatians 5 :19-21).

18. "*The fruit of the Spirit is love, joy, peace, patience, kindness, goodness, faithfulness, gentleness and self-control. Against such things there is no law*" (Galatians 5 :22-23).

19. "*Those who belong to Christ Jesus have crucified the sinful nature with its passions and desires*" (Galatians 5 :24)

20. "*Put to death, therefore, whatever belongs to your earthly nature : sexual immorality, impurity, lust, evil desires and greed, which is idolatry*" (Colossians 3 :5).

21. "*But now you must rid yourselves of all such things as these : anger, rage, malice, slander and filthy language from your lips*" (Colossians 3 :8).

22. "*Do not lie to each other, since you have taken off your old self with its practices and have put on the new self, which is being renewed in knowledge in the image of its Creator*" (Colossians 3 :9-10).

23. "*Therefore, as God's chosen people, holy and dearly loved, clothe yourselves with compassion, kindness, humility, gentleness and patience. Bear with each other and forgive whatever grievances you may*

have against one another. Forgive as the Lord forgave you. And over all these virtues put on love, which binds them all together in perfect unity" (Colossians 3 :12-14).

24. "*For this very reason, make every effort to add to your faith goodness ; and to goodness, knowledge ; and to knowledge, self-control ; and to self-control, perseverance ; and to perseverance, godliness ; and to godliness, brotherly kindness ; and to brotherly kindness, love. For if you possess these qualities in increasing measure, they will keep you from being ineffective and unproductive in your knowledge of our Lord Jesus Christ*" (2 Peter 1 : 5-8).

THE MARKS OF SPIRITUAL BARRENNESS

Spiritual barrenness is manifested by one or more of the following:

1. No souls won for the Lord.
2. Fewer souls won in the present time than in past times.
3. The Gospel is preached to the lost without burden.
4. The Gospel is preached to the lost without zeal.
5. The people brought to the Lord do not abide.
6. The people brought to the Lord do not mature.
7. Fruit is borne at the present at the same rate as it was borne in the past.
8. There is no clear vision about the call of God with increasing time.
9. The word of God does not touch the heart as it did before.
10. The word of God touches the heart at the same level as before.
11. There is a lower capacity to obey God now than in the past.
12. The capacity to obey God has not increased with time.
13. Less time is given to God than in the past.

14. The same amount of time is given to the Lord now as in the past.
15. Time spent with the Lord leaves the person dry.
16. Time spent with the Lord leaves the person confused.
17. Lack of the power to pluck in to God.
18. More time is spent on self now than in the past.
19. The Bible is read less now than in the past.
20. Christian literature is read less now than in the past.
21. Less money is given to God now than in the past.
22. The same amount of money or the same percent of income is given to God now as in the past.
23. There is no increasing dying to self.
24. The talent that God gave the person has not been used for the glory of God.
25. The spiritual gift of the person has been used to exalt self.
26. The works of the flesh are not on the decrease in quality.
27. The works of the flesh are not on the decrease in quantity.
28. The fruit of the Spirit is not seen in increasing qualitative abundance.
29. The fruit of the Spirit is not seen in increasing quantitative abundance.
30. There is love of money in the heart.
31. There is love of the world in the heart.
32. There is love of pleasure in the heart.
33. The cares of the world : husband, wife, parents, children, success, fame, etc., are on the heart.
34. There are no labours to systematically put on more and more of the character of Christ.
35. There are no labours to put off more and more of the character of the devil.

36. Immaturity with increasing time

THE CAUSE OF SPIRITUAL BARRENNESS

There is one overriding cause of spiritual barrenness, and that is failure in relationship with the Lord; for fruit is the overflow of the relationship between a believer and his Lord. If the person has never been grafted on the true Vine ; if he has never been born from above, then it is impossible for him to produce any spiritual fruit. That one is dead, and corpses do not reproduce.

Secondly, fruit is directly proportional to union with the Lord. Where there is no union with the Lord, there will be no fruit. Where there is a small union, there will be little fruit. Where there is intimate union, there will be much fruit. Where the union is great, there will be great fruit. When union continues, fruit-bearing continues and when union ceases, fruit-bearing ceases.

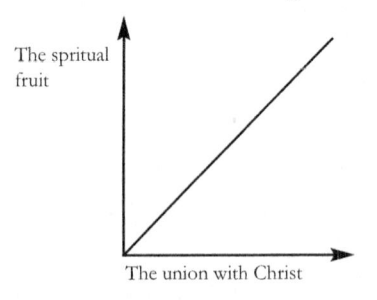

Y-axis: The spritual fruit; X-axis: The union with Christ

If a person is spiritually barren or if he is stagnant or if he has backslidden, there is only one reason - his relationship with the Lord. He may blame the environment, the system, the brethren, the lack of this and the lack of that. However, these are only secondary. The real problem is that something is wrong in his relationship with the Lord.

The Lord Jesus said, " *No branch can bear fruit by itself* " (John 15

:4).

"*You cannot bear fruit unless you remain in me*" (John 15 :4).

"*If a man remains in me and I in him, he will bear much fruit*" (John 15 :5).

If a person is in ever-increasing union with the Lord Jesus, he will bear ever-increasing fruit. There may be many adverse circumstances on the outside :
- persecution,
- financial shortages,
- hostile people,
- etc.

However, as long as the relationship with the Lord is what it should be, there will be abundant fruit.

Each one has only himself to blame for his spiritual barrenness. Those who are honest and own up to the fact that they are responsible will turn to the Lord, sort things with Him, get back to the right relationship with Him, and begin to bear fruit again. Those who blame one person or another, one circumstance or another for their barrenness will continue to be barren.

We insist that the cause of barrenness is a deficient relationship with the Lord Jesus, and only as the relationship is corrected with Him can fruitfulness ever be restored.

INTIMACY WITH THE LORD JESUS

There are a number of factors that could affect intimacy with Jesus . The first of them is the sin or sins committed. Any sin in

- desire
- thought
- look
- touch
- feeling
- taste
- word
- deed

that is known but not

- hated
- confessed
- abandoned

separates a person from the Lord Jesus. One such sin breaks the relationship with the Lord Jesus, and more and more sins only help to distance the person from the Lord Jesus. Anyone who has a sin separating him from the Lord Jesus has lost intimacy with Him, and until the situation is settled there can be no abiding fruit. In soul winning, someone with one sin in his life known but not confessed and not forsaken may carry out evangelism and apparently " lead many people to the Lord Jesus ". However, this is a waste of time. The apparent harvest is no harvest ! A tree may produce

- many flowers
- small fruit
- big fruit
- very big fruit

but none may ripen. None may mature. I have seen mango

- flowers

- small fruit
- big fruit
- very big fruit

fall to the ground at different stages. I have seen what looked like a very healthy mango fruit, but before it ripened it got rotten. I have seen what on the outside looked like a ripe, mature mango, but when it was harvested, there it was - rotten inside and not good enough to be eaten. Let no one deceive himself that with a sin known but not confessed and forsaken he is bearing fruit - no, he is wasting time. If the fruit cannot satisfy the heart of God, of what use is it?

My beloved, you know your heart. Can you bear fruit that is approved by God ? Are you wasting your time ? Are you producing fruit or are you producing apparent fruit ? You may deceive yourself now but remember, at the judgment seat of Christ what is produced by a heart with one or more sin will be shown to have been mere

- wood,
- hay,
- stubble,

that shall all be burnt by fire. Only that which is being produced by sin-free hearts will be tested and approved as having been

- gold,
- silver,
- precious stone.

Another factor that could affect intimacy with the Lord Jesus is malnutrition . Malnutrition could result from not eating the right type of food. For example, if someone remains on spiritual milk when he ought to be eating solid food, the relationship with the Lord

Jesus will be affected even if he drinks many gallons of milk a day. Also, if he eats solid food in insufficient quantity, he will not be healthy enough. For abiding fruit, for ever-increasing fruit, a person must give more and more of himself, spend more and more time with Jesus, study more and more of the word, give more and more of his substance and serve the Lord ever increasingly. Only such a life can continue to maintain the type of relationship that satisfies the heart of Jesus and thus flow forth in increasing fruit. There is the indispensable addition. The Apostle Peter wrote, "*His divine power has given us everything we need for life and godliness through our knowledge of him who called us by his own glory and goodness. Through these he has given us his very great and precious promises, so that through them you may participate in the divine nature and escape the corruption in the world caused by evil desires. For this very reason, make every effort to add to your faith, goodness ; and to goodness, knowledge; and to knowledge, self-control; and to self-control, perseverance ; and to perseverance, godliness ; and to godliness, brotherly kindness ; and to brotherly kindness , love. For if you possess these qualities in increasing measure, they will keep you from being ineffective and unproductive in your knowledge of our Lord Jesus Christ. But if anyone does not have them, he is near-sighted and blind, and has forgotten that he has been cleansed from his past sins*" (2 Peter 1 :3-9).

We can set this out as follows :

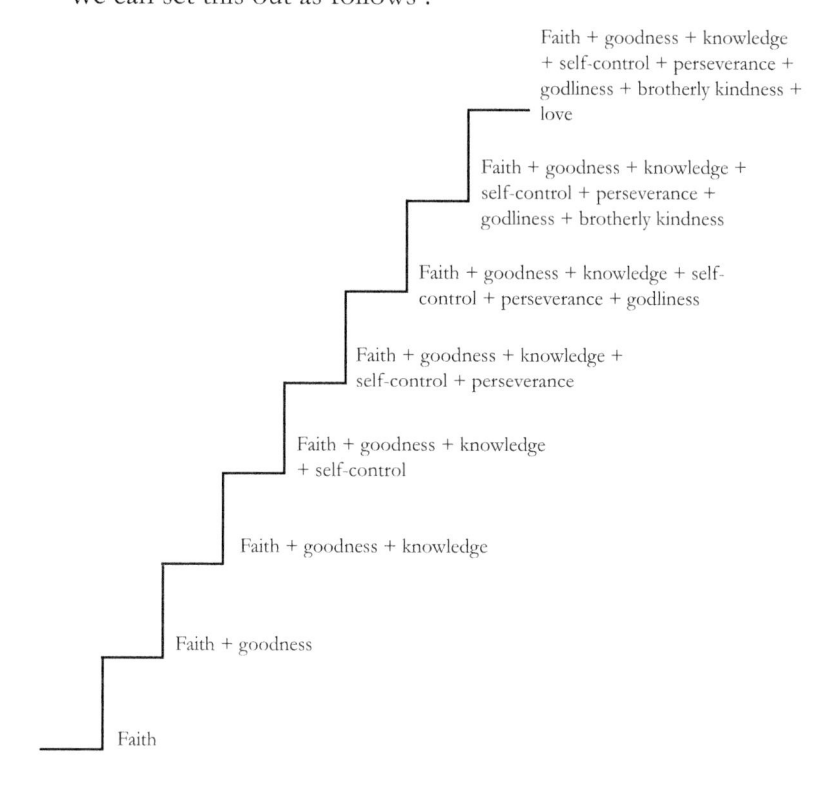

- Faith
- Faith + goodness
- Faith + goodness + knowledge
- Faith + goodness + knowledge + self-control
- Faith + goodness + knowledge + self-control + perseverance
- Faith + goodness + knowledge + self-control + perseverance + godliness
- Faith + goodness + knowledge + self-control + perseverance + godliness + brotherly kindness
- Faith + goodness + knowledge + self-control + perseverance + godliness + brotherly kindness + love

Everything being equal, we ought to be able to tell the age of a believer from what he has put on. Unfortunately, this is not so. It is not so because a barren believer of 20 years standing might not have more put on than a committed believer of three years standing.

So the person who as a spiritual babe is admitted into the Lord's presence and drawn into intimacy with Him must continue to grow and to put on Christ for the relationship to continue . A parent joyfully carries his infant baby of a few weeks or months and is pleased as the baby smiles back to him . However, if after five years the child has not grown and made progress, it will cease to be a joy to the parent and the intimacy that was there initially would be lost. Continued intimacy with the Lord demands continued growth on the part of the believer. Continued intimacy is directly proportional to continued growth.

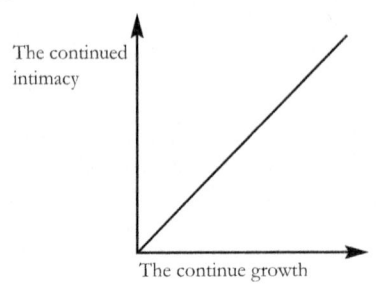

The continued intimacy (y-axis) vs. The continue growth (x-axis) — linear graph.

FRUITFULNESS AND PRAYER

The Lord Jesus said, "*If you remain in me and my words remain in you, ask whatever you wish and it will be given to you*" (John 15 :7). We conclude from these words of our Lord that intimacy leads to prayer that God answers. This means that a person who does not abide in the Lord ; that is a person who is not intimate with the Lord, may pray but his prayers will not be answered. Isaiah proclaimed, "*Surely the arm of the Lord is not too short to save, nor his ear too dull to hear. But your iniquities have separated you from your God ; your sins have hidden his face from you, so that he will not hear*" (Isaiah 59 :1-2).

The way to fruitfulness is by asking in prayer. However, only those who ask from intimacy in which every sin that separated them from the Lord has been removed can ask and receive.

We can say, therefore, that prayer is the way to intimacy with the Lord, because during prayer the heart is laid bare before God and every sin is exposed. If it is then removed through confession and forsaking, union with the Lord is established or re-established. Also, during prayer, areas of weaknesses are exposed by the Holy Spirit to the praying believer. If in return these are made objects of prayer, the Lord will in answer remove the weaknesses. With sins removed, weaknesses removed, undeveloped areas developed, a fuller union with the Lord is entered into, and from that fuller union prayer is offered to the Lord at a higher dimension. This moves God to do things that those who do not know that dimension of union with Him cannot move Him to do.

We can, therefore, say that Prayer enables a man to become intimate with God. That person who is intimate with God will pray prayers that will move God to produce in his life and through his life fruit that satisfies God.

We conclude that fruitfulness is dependent on the quantity and quality of prayer.

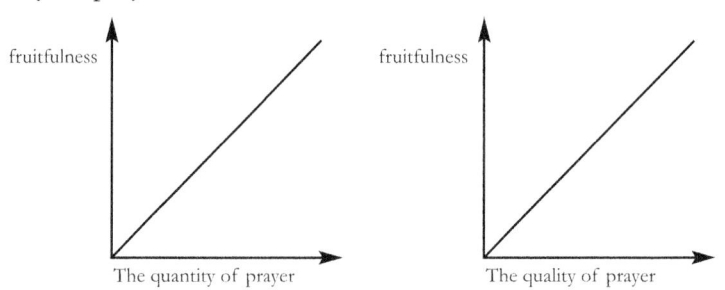

[Two line graphs: left graph shows fruitfulness (y-axis) vs. The quantity of prayer (x-axis); right graph shows fruitfulness (y-axis) vs. The quality of prayer (x-axis). Both show a linear positive relationship.]

For those who want to bear much fruit and thus satisfy the heart of God, there is no substitute for abundant prayer from deepest intimacy with God. Such will wait before God in prayer so that God will X-ray their hearts and show them what is wrong in them. During the X-ray, the Holy Spirit will show one thing and, as they repent and forsake it and carry out the needed restitution, He will show them the next; and as they repent, forsake the sin and carry out the needed restitution, He will show them the next. This will go on and on and on for as long as there are barriers between the person and God and as long as the person is prepared to repent, forsake the sin and carry out restitution. If the X-ray shows that there is a particular sin in the heart and life of the person being X-rayed and the person does not confess it and part with it at once, the Lord will stop the X-raying there and the person can go on without deepest union with God. This can continue indefinitely. If, on the other hand, the person keeps confessing and forsaking each sin that the Lord shows him in the X-ray, the Lord will continue until a time comes when there is no more sin left in that life.

When that point is reached, the person can begin to pray for fruit to be produced in his life and through his life. He can continue to pray and pray and, the more he prays, the more the Lord will answer and the more there will be fruit.

That person will also pray for others and the Lord will hear his prayers and bring the persons to deep repentance, radical forsaking of sin and far-reaching restitutions that will precede a far-reaching prayer life that will yield much fruit.

So a chain can be started and continue to the glory of God and the blessing of man. We can present it as follows:

Believer A undergoes the X-ray of God and continues to confess and forsake all his sins as they are shown to him, until the Lord shows him that there is nothing more to confess and forsake.

Believer A who is pure asks and is filled with the Holy Spirit and continues to walk in utter purity before God, confessing and forsaking the slightest sin that is revealed at once ; so that there is no break in the flow of the Holy Spirit.

Believer A begins to pray abundantly and intensely for fruit to be produced in and through his life in abundance, and God begins to answer abundantly.

Believer A begins to pray that the Holy Spirit should do in Believer B all that He has done in him step by step, and that Believer B should come through without resisting God anywhere. In answer to the abundant, powerful, and persistent prayers of Spirit-filled Believer A, Believer B co-operates fully with God in everything until he is transformed into a Spirit-filled believer who now prays abundant, powerful and persistent prayers for fruit in his life and for the Lord's work in Believer C.

So at this point we have two Spirit-filled believers - Believer A and Believer B. Both are continuing to walk in radical purity and complete fullness of the Holy Spirit. Both are praying abundantly, powerfully and persistently for abundant fruitfulness in their lives and through their lives. In addition, Believer A is praying that God should do what He has done in his life in Believer D, while Believer B is praying that God should do what He has done in his life in Believer C. Believer A and Believer B will wrestle with God - giving Him no rest and taking no rest - until God does a deep and total work in Believer C and Believer D. They will press on in prayer and refuse to be satisfied with the beginnings of the work or the advancement of the work. They will press on and on until the Lord assures them that the work in Believer C and in Believer D has been carried out to His satisfaction . The Bible says, " *I have posted watchmen on your walls, O Jerusalem ; they will never be silent day or night. You who call on the Lord, give yourselves no rest, and give him no rest till he establishes Jerusalem and makes her the praise of the earth* " (Isaiah 62 :6-7).

This is the pathway to fruitfulness at the personal level and the pathway to fruitfulness at the corporate level. This is the pathway to personal revival and the pathway to corporate revival.

Prayer is the way to perfect personal purity of heart and life.

Prayer is the way to perfect personal consecration of life and all to the Lord.

Prayer is the way to perfect personal freedom from the self-life.

Prayer is the way to perfect personal freedom from the love of the world.

Prayer is the way to perfect personal freedom from the love of anything in the world.

Prayer is the way to bring another believer into perfect personal purity of heart and life, perfect personal consecration of life and all to the Lord, perfect personal freedom from the self-life, perfect personal freedom from the love of the world, perfect personal freedom from the love of anything in the world.

Prayer is the way to a supreme love of God with spirit, soul and body. Prayer is the way to bring another believer to a supreme love of God with spirit, soul and body.

Prayer is the way to a supreme love of the sinners that Jesus died to save. Prayer is the way to a supreme investment of life and all into the salvation of the sinners that Jesus died to save.

Prayer is the way to move another believer to a supreme love of the sinners that Jesus died to save. Prayer is the way to move another believer to a supreme investment of a life and all into the salvation of the sinners that Jesus came to save.

Prayer is the way to supremacy with God and man.

God says, " *Ask of me, and I will make the nations your inheritance, the ends of the earth your possession* " (Psalm 2 :8).

BARRENNESS IS A PERSONAL CHOICE

Because prayer is the way out of barrenness into fruitfulness and because everyone who wants to pray can pray, anyone who is barren and continues to be barren is in that condition by personal choice !

There is nothing that God can do for the one who has chosen to be barren ! !

You can set out to end your barrenness today !

FRUITFULNESS IS A PERSONAL CHOICE

End your barrenness today and begin to bear fruit !
Act now ! !
Take the first step now ! ! !
God bless you ! ! ! !

CHAPTER 6

THE PHYSICAL BARRENNESS OF HANNAH

PHYSICAL BARRENNESS

It is expected that a married woman should conceive and give birth to children. A woman could be married but not give birth to children because of one of the following reasons :

1. She and the husband have decided not to have children.
2. She is sick in her reproductive system.
3. An organ in her reproductive system remained undeveloped.
4. Her husband lacks the power to make a woman pregnant.
5. She and her husband are healthy but the Lord closed her womb.

HANNAH WAS BARREN

The Bible says, *"He (Elkanah) had two wives ; one was called Hannah and the other Peninnah. Peninnah had children, but Hannah had none"* (1 Samuel 1 :2). It was obvious that Hannah's barrenness was not because she and her husband had decided not to have children. It was also obvious that the fault was not with her husband. The problem was with her.

In order to know how she should have felt, it is good to see how another woman in the same type of situation felt. The Bible says of Rachel, *"When Rachel saw that she was not bearing Jacob any children, she became jealous of her sister. So she said to Jacob, 'Give me children, or I'll die'"* (Genesis 30.1). When God opened her womb, the Bible says, *" Then God remembered Rachel; he listened to her and opened her womb. She became pregnant and gave birth to a son and said, ' God has taken away my disgrace '"* (Genesis 30 :22-23).

Rachel felt so desperate about her barrenness that she would have preferred death to being barren. She was in a constant state of disgrace.

BARRENNESS NOT A BLESSING

The Bible generally portrays barrenness as a condition of God's disfavour. The blessings for obedience included: *"The fruit of your womb will be blessed"* (Deuteronomy 28:4). The curses for disobedience also included: *"The fruit of your womb will be cursed"* (Deuteronomy 28:28). Michal despised David for dancing before the Lord and reaped the punishment of having no children to the day of her death (2 Samuel 6:23).

The Bible continues to say: *" If a man sleeps with his aunt, he has dishonoured his uncle. They will be held responsible, they will die childless"* (Leviticus 20:20). *" If a man marries his brother's wife, it is an act of impurity, he has dishonoured his brother. They will be childless"* (Leviticus 20:21).

HANNAH: BARREN, DISTURBED BUT NOT DESPERATE

Hannah was barren. It was obvious that her barrenness was her fault, since her husband had children with his other wife. She ought to have been deeply troubled; she ought to have lived in a state of disgrace. Strangely enough, Hannah was not desperate. She did not cry out to God. She did not cry out desperately to God. She went on as if all was not too bad even though she was barren.

What caused Hannah not to confront the reality of her barrenness? The Bible says, *" Year after year this man went up from his town to worship and sacrifice to the Lord Almighty at Shiloh, where Hophni and Phinehas, the two sons of Eli, were priests of the Lord. Whenever the day came for Elkanah to sacrifice, he would give portions of the meat to his wife Peninnah and to all her sons and daughters. But to Hannah he gave a double portion because he loved her"* (1 Samuel 1:3-5).

Hannah was deceived by the love of Elkanah !

Hannah was deceived by the double portions of meat ! !

Because she allowed herself to be deceived , she was fairly content in her barren condition. Because she allowed herself to receive some satisfaction from a husband's love and a double portion of meat, she was shielded from the full weight of her barren condition.

ARE YOU BARREN BUT NOT DESPERATE?

Are you barren in
- intimacy with Christ,
- the fruit of the Spirit,
- spiritual gifts,
- souls brought to the Lord,
- many other ways,

and yet you are undisturbed ?

What has deceived you ?

Is it your financial situation that is comfortable?

Is it your good marriage?

Is it a leadership title even though you do not deserve it and there is nothing to back it ?

Is it some deceitful praise that you are a fabulous evangelist because people do come forward in your crusades even though they do not abide ?

Is it the deception that all believers will be in heaven and that all will be perfectly happy and consequently there is no reason to worry ?

Is it the deception that even though you may have no works that will survive the test of fire, you will nevertheless be saved and that that is all that matters ?

Is it the deception that because you cannot lose your salvation all is alright and all will be alright in the future regardless of what you do ?

<u>Hannah was deceived for some time. Hers was an unusual barrenness for some time ! However, she was not permanently unusually barren !</u>

<u>We do hope your own deception comes to an end soon!</u>

THE DECEITFULNESS OF THINGS

Hannah was barren but not desperate because she had a double portion of meat. Meat provided some satisfaction and so stood in her way of turning desperately to God. She also had her husband's love. Meat and a husband's love appear legitimate. The only problem is that the legitimate things of this world crowd the heart and weaken the desire for the Lord Jesus.

Hannah was not distracted from desperately seeking the Lord by some very ugly sins. She was distracted by what was permitted. The Lord Jesus said, " *Still others, like seed sown among thorns, hear the word ; but the worries of this life, the deceitfulness of wealth and the desires for other things come in and choke the word, making it unfruitful* " (Mark 4 :18-19).

In Hannah's heart there was a place for her need of a child to be nursed to maturity. However, a part of that space in her heart was occupied by meat and her husband's love. This reduced the intensity with which she could have sought a solution to her need.

Nothing is neutral. Everything of this world seeks to occupy a place in the heart of man. Another shirt, another tie, another pair of trousers, another pair of shoes, and you are not quite the same. Your heart has lost something of its power to hunger for Jesus. Jesus asked the rich young ruler to go and sell all that he possessed and give the money to the poor and he would have treasures in heaven. Then he would come and follow Him. The rich young ruler wanted to follow Jesus and keep his wealth, but because it was not possible, Jesus asked him to part with his wealth, and then come follow Him. Jesus knew that no one could keep his wealth and follow Jesus, because his heart would be divided. Jesus demanded that those who would follow Him should part with or give up all that they possessed. The Bible says, *"In the same way, any of you who does not give up everything he has cannot be my disciple"* (Luke 14:33).

The things of this world choke the desire for God from the human heart. Those who are wise are suspicious of the things of the world. They fear everything in this world. They touch the things of the world and use them with fear and trembling, lest these things choke the desire to bear fruit for the Lord. They touch the things of the world with fear and trembling, lest these things distract them from a wholehearted devotion to the Lord.

Everything of the world :
- a bigger salary,
- a more elevated position,
- a bigger certificate,
- a bigger car,
- a bigger house,
- etc,

destroys spiritual hunger and comforts people in their barrenness. This is sad indeed. It is very sad.

The Apostle Paul wrote, "*But whatever was to my profit I now consider loss for the sake of Christ. What is more, I consider everything a loss compared to the surpassing greatness of knowing Christ Jesus my Lord, for whose sake I have lost all things. I consider them rubbish, that I may gain Christ*" (Philippians 3:7-8).

CHAPTER 7

THE MINISTRY OF PROVOCATION

THE MINISTRY OF PROVOCATION

The ministry of provocation is that of stirring a person into doing something which he would normally not do if the provocation did not come. It is encouraging someone to do that which he can do but is not doing. It is pressuring someone to do that which he could do but has not done. The goal of the ministry of provocation is to ensure that something God wants done is done.

In the case of Hannah, Peninnah was the minister of provocation. We do not know what her motives were. All we can say is that she provoked Hannah to act and her action, resulting from the provocation, caused God's glory to be established. The Bible says, " Year after year this man went up from his town to worship and sacrifice to the Lord Almighty at Shiloh, where Hophni and Phinehas, the two sons of Eli, were priests of the Lord. Whenever the day came for Elkanah to sacrifice, he would give portions of the meat to his wife Peninnah and to all her sons and daughters. But to Hannah he gave a double portion because he loved her, and the Lord had closed her womb. And because the Lord had closed her womb, her rival kept provoking her in order to irritate her. This went on year after year. Whenever Hannah went up to the house of the Lord, her rival provoked her till she wept and would not eat. Elkanah her husband would say to her, ' Hannah, why are you weeping ? Why don't you eat ? Why are you downhearted ? Don't I mean more to you than ten sons ? ' " (1 Samuel 1 :3-8).

Could it be that Peninnah saw that Hannah would have a child if only she cried out desperately to the Lord ? Could it be that she saw that the nation needed a prophet and that none of her own sons could ever become the needed prophet ? Could it be that she saw in Hannah the qualities that could make her the mother of a prophet ? Could it be that God revealed to her that Hannah's son would one day be the nation's prophet ? Was it mere female jealousy that led her to become the minister of provocation for Hannah? We do not know exactly what motivated her to function in the capacity of a minister of provocation. We, however, know that she carried out the ministry well and succeeded!

She might have said something like the following: "Hannah, do not be content with meat. Do not be content with a double portion of meat. A double portion of meat is not a child. Cry out to God for a child."

At another opportunity, she might perhaps have said, " Hannah, a husband's love is not a baby. Many women are loved by their husbands and they have babies also. Hannah, you are barren. God has closed your womb. Cry out to Him so that He should open your womb and give you a child."

It could be that Peninnah was ignored by Hannah from the beginning but she continued. The Bible says that Peninnah kept provoking her in order to irritate her. She possibly wanted to irritate her so that in her irritation she would cry out to God for help.

The Bible says that this went on year after year until she wept and would not eat. The ministry of provocation continued year after year. The minister of provocation was looking for results and, as long as there were no results, she kept pressing on.

SELF-PITY

The first reaction of Hannah to the ministry of provocation, which she was receiving, was self-pity. The Bible says that she wept and would not eat.

Weeping can be a blessing and fasting can be a blessing, if these two are God-centred. They can be a blessing if they are an overflow of the heart towards God. However, for Hannah they were just an expression of wounded pride : an expression of self-pity. The tears flowed from self and flowed to self. The refusal to eat was self-pity. The ministry of provocation had not yet accomplished its goal.

There is a lot of weeping by saints which is just self-pity. There is a lot of fasting that is just a manifestation of self. The weeping that is effective is that which is crying out to God. That kind of weeping moves God, but self-centred weeping is useless. The following is said about Esau : " *See that no one is sexually immoral, or is godless like Esau, who for a single meal sold his inheritance rights as the oldest son. Afterwards, as you know, when he wanted to inherit this blessing, he was rejected. He could bring about no change of mind, though he sought the blessing with tears* " (Hebrews 12 :16-17).

Hannah wept, but there was no turning to God. God did not see her tears. Her husband saw them and tried to console her. He said, " *Hannah, why are you weeping ? Why don't you eat ? Why are you downhearted ? Don't I mean more to you than ten sons ?*" (1 Samuel 1 :8).

He was trying to encourage her to continue in her barren condition. He asked if he did not mean more to her than ten sons ! The truth is that she had a husband and she needed children and there was no way in which her barrenness could be compensated for by her having a husband. The minister of provocation might have told her, " Hannah, do not allow yourself to be deceived. A husband is not a substitute for children. You need children. Do not be satisfied with empty words."

Peninnah continued to provoke Hannah until she abandoned self-pity and turned to God. She had succeeded. The Bible says, "*Once when they had finished eating and drinking in Shiloh, Hannah stood up. Now Eli the priest was sitting on a chair by the doorpost of the Lord's temple. In bitterness of soul Hannah wept much and prayed to the Lord*" (1 Samuel 1:9-10).

The ministry of provocation has as its goal to turn complacent people or those filled with self-pity to confront their problem squarely by bringing it to God in prayer, or by acting in such a way that the problem will be solved God's way.

MINISTERS OF PROVOCATION

I believe that there is a need of many ministers of provocation today. Such will take no rest until they have shaken lazy believers out of their laziness. They will take no rest until they have shaken immature believers out of their immaturity. They will take no rest until they have provoked the believers who are doing well to do better, and those who are doing better to do their best!

Everyone who is barren needs a ministry of provocation. Those who are doing very well need a ministry of provocation. All is done to press the believer to become his best. What the believer has accomplished is wisely compared with what he could have accomplished.

The Apostle Paul was ministering as a minister of provocation when he wrote the following to the Corinthians, "*And now, brothers, we want you to know about the grace that God has given the Macedonian churches. Out of the most severe trial, their overflowing joy and their extreme poverty welled up in rich generosity. For I testify that they gave as much as they were able, and even beyond their ability. Entirely on their own, they urgently pleaded with us for the privilege of sharing in this service to the saints. And they did not do as we expected, but they gave themselves first to the Lord and then to us in keeping with God's will. So we urged Titus, since he had earlier made a beginning, to bring also to completion this act of grace on your part. But just as you excel in everything - in faith, in speech, in knowledge, in complete earnestness and in your love for us - see that you also excel in this grace of giving"* (2 Corinthians 8:1-7). Here the apostle was lovingly and gently provoking the brethren to do an excelling job. This is the ministry of provocation.

CARRYING OUT THE MINISTRY OF PROVOCATION

In carrying out the ministry of provocation the wiser ministers of provocation can gently and tenderly provoke the person to do what should be done by wisely stirring the person to do his best or by gentle comparison with another person. This will move the person to act without being hurt. This is much better and we encourage people to carry out the ministry of provocation along those lines.

However, there are some people who are very stubborn and will not be moved by gentle provocation. Such need to be handled more roughly. Sharp words of provocation need to be brought in to shake the person out of his laziness into action.

I remember that in my 4th year in the Primary School I came home weeping with my end of term results because I was the second in my class. My father saw me weeping and coming home. He asked me why I was weeping. I told him that I was the second in the class. He said, " Second ! Oh, then you have failed. " I wept even more, but his provocation was effective. The next term I was back to the top of the class and remained there until I completed from the Primary School. It was not gentle provocation but it was effective provocation.

I believe that I am in the ministry of provocation. Let me try and provoke you a little.

You are a child of God. That is wonderful. How long have you been in Christ ?

1. How many times have you read your Bible from Genesis to Revelation ? Have you read it one time for every year that you have been in the Lord ? This is the accepted average for average Christians. If you have not read it through every year (that is an average of three chapters a day), then you have been very lazy. Wake up from your slumber and catch up by reading six chapters everyday. You must know the Word in order to obey it.

2. Put away your Bible and write down the Scriptures that you have memorized, quoting the Book of the Bible , the chapter and the verse. Go on until you have written down all that you have memorized. How big is the Bible in your memory ? How many verses are accurate in reference and content ? If you are a normal believer, you should have memorized one verse a week. This means fifty verses a year. This means 500 verses in ten years. If you do not accurately memorize one verse a week, you are dangerously lazy. Wake up from your laziness and work . Work hard. Work harder. Work hardest !

3. Write down the Bible in your life. Any command or example of the Bible that you have obeyed consistently until it has become a part of your life is the Bible in your life. For example, the Bible says, " *You shall not murder* " (Exodus 20 :13). If you do not murder in deed, words or thoughts, if there is no-one

(not even a political leader) whom you occasionally wish dead ; if you hate no-one (for hatred is murder), then write down : " You shall not murder " in your Bible. The Bible says , " *You shall not commit adultery* " (Exodus 20 :14). If over the last twelve months or more you have not committed adultery or fornication in desire, thought, look, touch, word or act, then write down : " You shall not commit adultery " as a part of your Bible. A third example is " *You shall not steal* " (Exodus 20 :15). If you have not stolen from God, from man, from your government (in false or crooked tax or customs declaration), from your employer (time, money, telephone calls for personal issues, etc) ; if you have given to God regularly and faithfully since you believed, etc, then write down : " You shall not steal . " Go on and on and see how much of the Bible is written in your life. The only Bible you will take with you when you leave this world will be the Bible in your life, and that will affect your eternal rank significantly.

4. Write down how much money you have earned in your life. Write down how much money you have already sent ahead into your heavenly account. To spend more money on your needs, wants and luxuries during the eighty to one hundred years that you will live in this world and to provide very little for the time you will live in heaven is great folly. The Bible says, " *Do not store up for yourselves treasures on earth, where moth and rust destroy, and where thieves break in and steal. But store up for yourselves treasures in heaven, where moth and rust do not destroy, and where thieves do not break in and steal. For where your treasure is there your heart will be also* " (Matthew 6 :19-21). Keep accurate accounts as to how much money you have already sent to heaven through investments into the perishing souls of men.

5. Is there any of the following sins in your life ? If there is any,

you will go to hell unless you repent and forsake it, and the safest time to forsake it is now. "*Do you not know that the wicked will not inherit the kingdom of God ? Do not be deceived : Neither the sexually immoral nor idolaters nor adulterers nor male prostitutes nor homosexual offenders nor thieves nor the greedy nor drunkards nor slanderers nor swindlers will inherit the kingdom of God*" (1 Corinthians 6 :9-10).

CHAPTER 8

THE BATTLE TO GIVE GOD A PROPHET FOR ISRAEL: A VISION OF GOD'S BURDEN

WHAT PRAYER IS

1. Prayer is to let Jesus into our needs.
2. To pray is to give Jesus permission to employ His power in the alleviation of our distress.
3. To pray is to let Jesus glorify His name in the midst of our needs.
4. To pray is to open the door, giving Jesus access to our needs and permitting Him to exercise His own power in dealing with them.
5. To pray is to verbalize our total dependence on God concerning all our efforts.
6. Prayer is the language of a man burdened with a sense of need. It is the voice of the beggar, conscious of his poverty, asking of another the things he needs. Not to pray is not only to declare there is nothing needed, but to admit to a non-realization of that need " (E.M.Bounds).
7. Prayer means that we have come boldly into the throne room and we are standing in His presence. It is more than bringing Him on the scene. It is going into the presence of the Father and Jesus in an executive meeting, laying our needs before them and making our requisitions for ability, for grace, for healing for someone , for victory for someone, or for financial needs " (E.M. Kenyon).
8. " When you have a desire or need for something, be it a commodity or a service, tangible or intangible, you make contact with a person or firm you presume could give you satisfaction. What follows is termed ' doing business' with them. Prayer is 'doing business' with God, and is every bit as practical as any earthly transaction " (Virginia Whitman).
9. To pray is to make a demand on God's ability.
10. " It is God's desire to bring individuals and families into saving faith. It is God's desire to bring people out of addiction to

drugs, sex, money, status. It is God's desire to deliver people from racism, sexism, nationalism, consumerism. It is God's desire to harvest cities, bringing whole communities into Gospel fidelity.... Prayer is a crucial means for the fulfilment of these yearnings in the heart of God " (Richard Foster).

HANNAH'S NEED

Hannah needed a son so as to be like the other women. Although this need was there, she could go on with the need unsatisfied. Her rival provoked her and she was depressed and wept and would not eat. That went on for years. Things might have continued that way until she died. However, things did not continue that way. Something happened. What happened ? We suggest that God revealed His need of a prophet for the nation to Hannah ! She saw that if she had a son, this son would become a useful vessel for God. Immediately she saw this, she changed. She was not too disturbed with her barrenness when having a child would satisfy only her and her husband. When she saw that having a child would meet God's needs, she became different. Her desire for a son became a craving, a passion, a must. From that moment, she turned from self-pity to aggressive wrestling with God so that God should give her the son who would serve His purpose.

Could the lack of revelation be the reason why you are lukewarm ? Could that be the reason why you are under no special burden to pray ? Could it be because you do not see how your prayer can fulfil the burden on God's heart ?

GOD HAS BURDENS

The Lord Jesus taught His disciples to pray,
"Our Father in heaven,

hallowed be your name,
your kingdom come,
your will be done on earth as it is in heaven" (Matthew 6 : 9-10).

The hallowing of God's name, the coming of God's Kingdom and the doing of God's will on earth as it is in heaven constitute some of God's burdens. God indeed has burdens. The Lord Jesus said, " *Come to me, all you who are weary and burdened, and I will give you rest. Take my yoke upon you and learn from me, for I am gentle and humble in heart, and you will find rest for your souls. For my yoke is easy and my burden is light"* (Matthew 11 :28-29).

For those who walk with God, there comes a time when God reveals His burden to them and also reveals what they can do to discharge that burden. From that moment, they are not quite the same. They change radically. They become people with a consuming passion. They take no rest. They give God no rest until they have moved God to do all that He must do to ensure that His burden is discharged.

HANNAH'S NEED AND GOD'S NEED

There was a time when Hannah saw only her need. Then God revealed His need to her. She then put aside her own need and gave herself to labour in order to ensure that God's need was met.

God's need and Hannah's need were not one. Her need was for a son; God's need was for a prophet. Hannah could have said, "I will use God to meet my need." If she had thought that way, she would have failed completely. If she had thought that way, she would have tried to keep Samuel for herself when he came. We thank God that she abandoned her need totally so that she might satisfy His need.

There are those who rejoice to obey God because He has called them to do something which seems to be in the direction of their own desires. However, they cannot satisfy the heart of God and satisfy their own desires. The will of God and the will of man may have superficial resemblances, but they are always an eternity apart in reality. The will of God is from above. The will of man is from below. The will of God is from the Holy Spirit. The will of man is from the flesh. There is no meeting place for that which is from the Holy Spirit and that which is from the flesh. If anyone wants to do the will of God, he must overthrow his own will completely. The will of God has one desire - to exalt the Lord Jesus and to exalt Him alone. The will of the flesh has one goal - to exalt the flesh. There is an eternal divorce between the desire to exalt the Lord Jesus and the desire to exalt self.

CHAPTER 9

THE BATTLE TO GIVE GOD A PROPHET FOR ISRAEL : THE SEPARATION OF HANNAH FROM THE OTHERS

The Bible says, "*Once when they had finished eating and drinking in Shiloh, Hannah stood up. Now Eli the priest was sitting on a chair by the doorpost of the Lord's temple*" (1 Samuel 1 :9).

Elkanah, Peninnah and their children had no need . They also had not seen God's need. If Hannah had continued in their company, what she had seen of God's need would have become dim. Separation from them for the task of doing God's business was inevitable. She stood up and separated herself from them , thus separating herself unto God.

There are many things of the inner life that can only happen when those who have seen what God wants to do and are determined to co-operate with Him, separate themselves from those who have either not seen or who have decided not to see. There are many things that cannot happen unless there is separation.

For Jacob to become Israel, he first separated himself from all the members of his family. The Bible says, "*That night Jacob got up and took his two wives, his two maidservants and his eleven sons and crossed the ford of the Jabbok. After he had sent them across the stream, he sent over all his possessions. So Jacob was left alone, and a man wrestled with him till day break. When the man saw that he could not overpower him, he touched the socket of Jacob's hip so that his heap was wrenched as he wrestled with the man. Then the man said, 'Let me go, for it is daybreak.' But Jacob replied, 'I will not let you go unless you bless me.' The man asked him, ' What is your name ?' 'Jacob,' he answered. Then the man said, 'Your name will no longer be Jacob, but Israel, because you have struggled with God and with men and have overcome.' Jacob said, 'Please tell me your name. ' But he replied, ' Why do you ask my name ?' Then he blessed him there*" (Genesis 32 :22-29).

The Lord Jesus often separated Himself from the others in order to have communion in prayer with His Father. The Bible says,

"That evening after sunset the people brought to Jesus all the sick and demon possessed. The whole town gathered at the door, and Jesus healed many who had various diseases. He also drove out many demons, but he would not let the demons speak because they knew who he was. <u>Very early in the morning, while it was still dark, Jesus got up, left the house and went off to a solitary place, where he prayed.</u> Simon and his companions went to look for him, and when they found him, they exclaimed : 'Everyone is looking for you '" (Mark 1 :32-37). Again, the Bible says about our Lord, " *While Jesus was in one of the towns, a man came along who was covered with leprosy. When he saw Jesus, he fell with his face to the ground and begged him, ' Lord, if you are willing, you can make me clean. Jesus reached out his hand and touched the man. ' I am willing, he said, ' Be clean! And immediately the leprosy left him. Then Jesus ordered him , ' Don't tell anyone, but go, show yourself to the priest and offer the sacrifices that Moses commanded for your cleansing , as a testimony to them. Yet the news about him spread all the more, so that crowds of people came to hear him and to be healed of their sicknesses. <u>But Jesus often withdrew to lonely places and prayed</u>*" (Luke 5 :12-16). Again the Bible says, "*Jesus went out as usual to the Mount of Olives, and his disciples followed him. On reaching the place, he said to them, ' Pray that you will not fall into temptation. <u>He withdrew about a stone's throw beyond them, knelt down and prayed, ' Father, if you are willing, take this cup from me ; yet not my will but yours be done '</u>*" (Luke 22 :39-42).

Hannah saw the need of God. She bore God's burden. The rest of her family was carrying no burden. If she had stayed with them, she would have lost her burden. There are times when the Holy Spirit lays a burden that should be discharged in prayer upon a heart. The one who receives the burden should immediately separate himself from the others who do not have the burden and seek God through prayer. If that is done, the burden will grow, intensify and lead to more and more prayer, until the Lord's purpose for that burden is accomplished . If the person, on the other hand, continues in the company of those who have not received the burden, other things will come into his heart and the burden will be lost. We insist that a burden should be discharged as soon as possible. We insist that the one who has received a burden from the Lord should work at it as soon as possible, and this will often mean separation from some for some time.

It may appear impolite for you to withdraw from the company of loved ones so as to spend time in the presence of the Lord. However, the alternative is to displease God and please man. Each one must make that choice. Yes, it is ultimately a question of whether or not we are prepared to please God. If we have decided that God is our unnegotiable priority, then everyone and everything will readily be put aside to please Him.

Hannah stood up. She separated herself from the others. She separated herself unto God. She trod the pathway that leads to God's best and she received God's best.

Hallelujah! Amen!

CHAPTER 10

THE BATTLE TO GIVE GOD A PROPHET FOR ISRAEL : THE BITTERNESS OF SOUL OF HANNAH

" Prayer is the language of a person desperately burdened with a sense of deepest need. It is the language flowing from the heart unto God from a person who must have an answer or perish. "

" Lord, give me Scotland or take my life " (John Knox)

"*Oh, what a great sin these people have committed ! They have made themselves gods of gold. But now, please forgive their sin but if not, then blot me out of the book you have written*" (Exodus 32 :31-32). (Moses)

"*In the month of Nisan in the twentieth year of King Artaxerxes, when wine was brought for him, I took the wine and gave it to the king. I had not been sad in his presence before ; so the king asked me, ' Why does your face look so sad when you are not ill ? This can be nothing but sadness of heart.* ' *I was very much afraid, but I said to the king, ' May the king live forever! Why should my face not look sad when the city where my fathers are buried lies in ruins, and its gates have been destroyed by fire ? '* " (Nehemiah 2 :1-3).

HANNAH'S AGONY

Hannah was bearing the burden of the Lord. She was now welded to the burden of God. The spiritual condition of Israel made it an absolute necessity that a prophet be born. Eli, the high priest, had lost control of things. His sons were actively living in sin. The holiness of God's name was being violated. God's name, God's honour, God's holiness needed to be vindicated. A son was needed who would champion the cause of vindicating the Lord. That son had to come by her. In a way, she saw her barrenness as something standing in the way of God. She was preventing God from having the man He needed . She was preventing the nation from having the leader she needed. This touched her inner being. It brought pain to her. There was the pain that she felt because she was bearing

God's pain in the situation. There was the greater pain that she felt because she was not giving God the son that He needed as His solution to the problem.

When a person takes God's burden and makes God's burden his burden, then God's burden actually becomes his burden. He bears it as he would his own burden. He bears it with even greater agony because it is God's burden.

How can I illustrate this? If, for example, you are carrying one million dollars that are your own money, maybe you can afford to relax while the money is on you because, should it be lost, you alone would have lost money. However, should the million dollars belong to your leader, you would be most careful with it because of whom it belongs to. You would not dare to take the risk of having his money lost.

Hannah was fully identified with God's burden and, consequently, knew bitterness of soul when the burden remained undischarged.

The Lord's burden in our day is for a Bride for the Lamb that is without spot, without wrinkle and without blemish. The Lord's burden is that the Gospel should be preached to the whole world as a witness and then the end will come. Why is it that few, very few believers are in bitterness of soul as they labour for the Lord's burden to be discharged?

The first problem is that many are not carrying any burden at all. They are not involved. They do not care.

The second problem is that many of those who are carrying a burden are carrying their own burden. They may say that they are doing things for the Lord but the reality is that they are following the deceitfulness of their imaginations. They have not received God's burden. They cannot receive God's burden because they have not handed their own burdens to Him. Man's burdens include the desire to be rich, the desire to be admired by the opposite sex, the desire to be seen, the desire to be heard, the desire to be promoted, the desire to be consulted, the fear of being forgotten, and so on. The desires of the flesh in one form or the other, the love of the world, the love of the things that are in the world and the pride of life are some of the burdens of man. Anyone who carries these burdens, even in christian service, cannot carry the burden of the Lord. To carry the burden of the Lord, a person must cast all his burdens at the feet of the Lord Jesus and leave them there permanently. Thus freed of his own burdens, he may then ask and receive the Lord's burden and carry that burden for Him.

The Lord will not give His burden to someone who is carrying some burden that has been put on him by himself, by believers or by unbelievers. When God sees a man carrying the burden of his own making, out of love for him, He will leave him alone.

Are you carrying a burden that is not the Lord's burden ? Will you part with it so that God may put His burden on you ?

The third problem is that God's burden carried by people of varying intimacy with Him will weigh on them in varying degrees. Those who are most intimate with Him will know the weight of His burden at a level that those who are distant from Him cannot know. The pure in heart will know the weight of God's burden in a way that those who are not so pure in heart cannot know. So burden is directly proportional to intimacy with God.

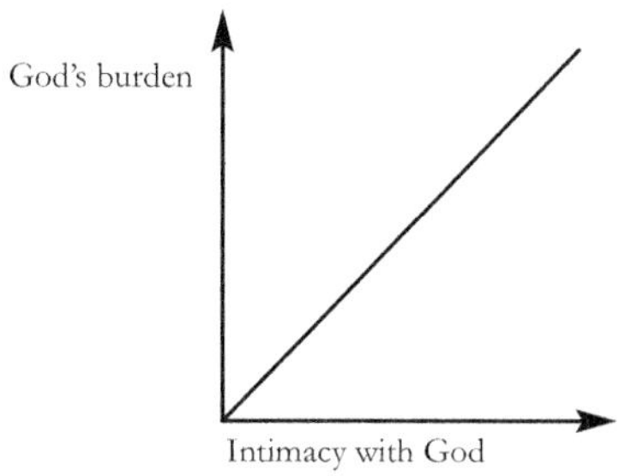

The more intimate a person is with the Lord, the more the Lord's burden will weigh on him.

Burden is also directly proportional to purity of heart. The purer a person's heart is, the more the Lord's burden will weigh upon him.

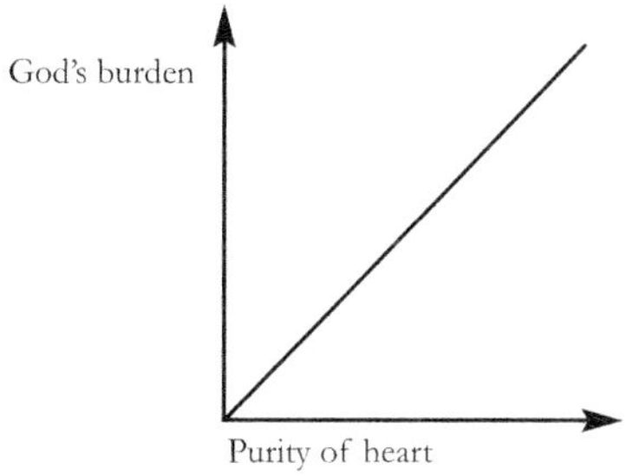

Burden is also directly proportional to consecration of life. The most radically consecrated carry a weight of the Lord's burden that the less consecrated cannot carry.

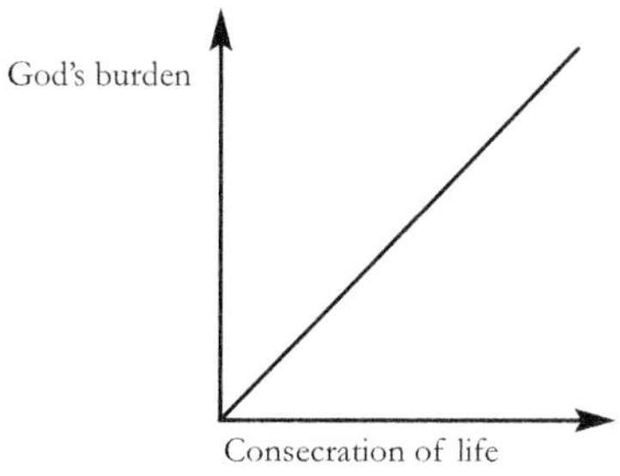

Hannah knew bitterness of soul about the Lord's burden. She

must have been intimate with the Lord. She must have been pure. She must have been consecrated to the Lord. In fact, seeing what happened when she prayed and what she did after her request was granted, we say without hesitation that she was intimate with God, pure in His sight and consecrated to Him.

How did this come about ? I believe that her many years of childlessness taught her to radically forsake
- sin,
- self,
- the love of the world,
- the love of the things of the world,

and draw close to Him. She had built intimacy with Him and so could receive His burden and carry it for Him.

Is there a major obstacle in your life ?

Are you barren ?

Are you handicapped ?

Is there a major cause of sorrow ?

Have you realised that God allowed these afflictions to come upon you so that you might turn more fully to Him ? Have you realized that He is using them to call you into a more intimate walk with Him ? Will you enter into intimacy with Him and thus give Him the opportunity to take away your burden ? When He will have taken away your burden, will you ask, receive and carry His own burden ? He invites you to Himself and He invites you to His burden.

Respond today !

Respond now ! !

CHAPTER 11

THE BATTLE TO GIVE GOD A PROPHET FOR ISRAEL : THE MUCH WEEPING OF HANNAH

"*Hannah wept much*" (1 Samuel 1:10).

What is it, this Prayer of Tears? It is being "cut to the heart" over our distance and offense to the goodness of God. It is weeping over our sins and the sins of the world. It is entering into the liberating shocks of repentance. It is the intimate and ultimate awareness that sin cuts us from the fullness of God's presence. (Richard J Foster)

My soul was exceedingly melted, and bitterly mourned over my exceeding sinfulness and vileness. I never before had felt so pungent and deep a sense of the odious nature of sin as at this time. My soul was then unusually carried forth in love to God and had a lively sense of God's love to me. (David Brainard)

Recently I experienced a special grace of the soft rain of tears. I had been considering my sin and the sins of God's people. I had also been meditating on the Gospel teaching (and the ancient teaching of the church) on "compunction" heart sorrow. As I did this, God graciously helped me enter into a holy mourning in my heart on behalf of the church and a deep tear-filled thanksgiving at God's patience, love, and mercy toward us. As Micah declares, "*Who is a God like you, pardoning iniquity?*" (Micah 7:18). For me this heart weeping lasted only a few days. I wish for more. These experiences seem to be the exception today; there was a time when they were the rule. It is reported of the French actress Eve La Vallière that after her conversion, her eyes were constantly irritated from perpetual weeping. (Richard J Foster)

"*My intercessor is my friend as my eyes pour out tears to God; on behalf of a man he pleads with God as a man pleads for his friend*" (Job 16:20-21).

" <u>So I weep</u>, as Jazer weeps, for the vines of Sibmah.
Heshbon, O Elealeh, <u>I drench you with tears</u> !
The shouts of joy over your ripened fruit
and over your harvests have been stilled.
Joy and gladness are taken away from the orchards ;
no-one sings or shouts in the vineyards ;
no-one treads out wine at the presses,
for I have put an end to the shouting.
<u>My heart laments</u> for Moab like a harp,
my inmost being for Kir Hareseth.
When Moab appears at her high place,
she only wears herself out ;
when she goes to her shrine to pray,
it is to no avail*" (Isaiah 16 :9-12).

" Oh , that my head were a spring of water
and my eyes a fountain of tears !
I would weep day and night for the slain of my people* " (Jeremiah 9 :1)

" I will weep and wail for the mountains
and take up a lament concerning the desert pastures.
They are desolate and untravelled,
and the lowing of cattle is not heard.
The birds of the air have fled
and the animals are gone " (Jeremiah 9 :10).

"Judah mourns,
her cities languish ;
They wail for the land,
and a cry goes up from Jerusalem " (Jeremiah 14 :2).

*" Let my eyes overflow with tears
night and day without ceasing;
for my virgin daughter my people
has suffered a grievous wound,
a crushing blow "* (Jeremiah 14 :17).

*" Weep and wail, you shepherds;
roll in the dust, you leaders of the flock.
For your time to be slaughtered has come ;
you will fall and be shattered like fine pottery "* (Jeremiah 25 :34).

*" I weep for you, as Jazer weeps,
O vines of Sibmah.
Your branches spread as far as the sea;
they reached as far as the sea of Jazer.
The destroyer has fallen on your ripened fruit and grapes "* (Jeremiah 48 :32).

*" The heart of the people cry out to the Lord.
O wall of the Daughter of Zion,
let your tears flow like a river day and night;
give yourself no relief, your eyes no rest.
Arise, cry out in the night, as the watches of the night begin;
pour out your heart like water in the presence of the Lord.
Lift up your hands to him for the lives of your children,
who faint from hunger at the head of every street "* (Lamentations 2 :18-19).

*" I am worn out from groaning;
all night long I flood my bed with weeping*

and drench my couch with tears.

My eyes grow weak with sorrow ; they fail because of all my foes" (Psalm 6 :6-7).

" As the deer pants for streams of water,
so my soul pants for you, O God.
My soul thirsts for God, for the living God.
When can I go and meet with God ?
My tears have been my food day and night,
while men say to me all day long,
' Where is your God ? '
These things I remember as I pour out my soul :
how I used to go with the multitude,
leading the procession to the house of God,
with shouts of joy and thanksgiving among the festive throng " (Psalm 42 :1-4).

" Record my lament ; list my tears on your scroll
are they not in your record ?
Then my enemies will turn back when I call for help.
By this I will know that God is for me " (Psalm 56 :8-9).

" Make your face shine upon your servant
and teach me your decrees.
Streams of tears flow from my eyes,
for your law is not obeyed " (Psalm 119 :135-136).

" When I heard these things, I sat down and wept. For some days I mourned and fasted and prayed before the God of heaven " (Nehemiah 1 : 4).

" In those days Hezekiah became ill and was at the point of death. The prophet Isaiah son of Amoz went to him and said, ' This is what the Lord says : Put your house in order, because you are going to die ; you will not recover. Hezekiah turned his face to the wall and prayed to the Lord, ' Remember, O Lord, how I have walked before you faithfully and with wholehearted devotion and have done what is good in your eyes. <u>And Hezekiah wept bitterly</u>. Then the word of the Lord came to Isaiah : ' Go and tell Hezekiah, This is what the Lord, the God of your father David, says : <u>I have heard your prayer and seen your tears</u> ; I will add fifteen years to your life. And I will deliver you and this city from the hand of the king of Assyria. I will defend this city " (Isaiah 38 :1-6).

" Put on sackcloth, O priests, and mourn;
wail, you who minister before the altar.
Come, spend the night in sackcloth,
you who minister before my God;
For the grain offerings and drink offerings
are withheld from the house of your God.
Declare a holy fast ; call a sacred assembly.
Summon the elders and all who live in the land
to the house of the Lord your God,
 and cry out to the Lord " (Joel 1 :13-14).

" ' Even now, ' declares the Lord, ' return to me with all your heart, with fasting and weeping and mourning. '

' Rend your heart and not your garments.

Return to the Lord your God, for he is gracious and compassionate, slow to anger and abounding in love, and he relents from sending calamity' " (Joel 2 :12-13).

" Blessed are those who mourn, for they shall be comforted " (Matthew 5 :4).

" *Blessed are you who hunger now, for you will be satisfied. Blessed are you who weep now, for you will laugh* " (Luke 6 :21).

" Now one of the Pharisees invited Jesus to have dinner with him, so he went to the Pharisee's house and reclined at the table. When a woman who had lived a sinful life in that town learned that Jesus was eating at the Pharisee's house, she brought an alabaster jar of perfume, and as she stood behind him at his feet weeping, she began to wet his feet with her tears. Then she wiped them with her hair, kissed them and poured perfume on them " (Luke 7 :36-38).

" I wrote you out of great distress and anguish of heart and with many tears, not to grieve you but to let you know the depth of my love for you " (2 Corinthians 2 :4).

" I served the Lord with great humility and with tears, although I was severely tested by the plot of the Jews " (Acts 20 :19).

" So be on your guard ! Remember that for three years I never stopped warning each of you night and day with tears"
(Acts 21 :31).

During the days of Jesus' life on earth, he offered up prayers and petitions with loud cries and tears to the one who could save him from death, and he was heard because of his reverent submission " (Hebrews 5:7).

The Bible is a book of weeping; a book of tears.

Why did Hannah weep? The following give us clues:
" *Tears are like blood in the wounds of the soul* " (Gregory of Nyssa.)

" Through the Prayer of Tears we give God permission to show us our sinfulness and the sinfulness of the world at the emotional level. As best as I can discern, tears are God's way of helping us descend with the mind into the heart and there bow in perpetual adoration and worship " (Richard J. Foster.)

" *Those who sow in tears will reap with songs of joy.*
He who goes out weeping, carrying seed to sow,
will return with songs of joy carrying, sheaves with him " (Psalms 126:5-6).

Hannah was sowing in tears, no wonder she reaped with songs of joy.

The poet, Phineas Fletcher wrote:

"Drop, drop, slow tears,
And bathe those beauteous feet,
Which brought from heaven
The news and Prince of peace.

Cease not, wet eyes,
His mercies to entreat;
To cry for vengeance
Sin doth never cease.

In your deep floods
Drown all my faults and fears;
Nor let his eye
See sin, but through my tears. "

Quotations marked Richard J Foster are from "Prayer : Finding The Heart's True Horn " by Richard J Foster, Harper Collins Publishers, 10 East 53rd Street, New York, NY 10022. USA.

CHAPTER 12

THE BATTLE TO GIVE GOD A PROPHET FOR ISRAEL : THE FASTING OF HANNAH

FASTING - 1

1. Fasting is the abstention from food for spiritual reasons.
2. Fasting softens the heart so that the things in it that God does not want can easily be uprooted.
3. Fasting softens the heart so that the things that need to be planted into the heart can easily germinate.
4. Fasting clarifies the mind so that things about which there was confusion are more readily sorted out.
5. Fasting causes the heart of the one fasting to be more sensitive towards God.
6. Fasting enables the heart to tilt more readily towards God's will.
7. Fasting makes it easier to believe God.
8. Fasting makes it easier to believe God's Word.
9. Fasting strengthens spiritual authority.
10. Fasting increases spiritual sight.
11. Fasting weakens the grip of the world on the heart.
12. Fasting weakens the grip of the things of the world on the heart.
13. Fasting reduces the heart's sensitivity to carnal feelings of hurt.
14. Fasting sharpens the capacity for spiritual correctness.
15. Fasting stirs the heart to love God.
16. Fasting stirs the heart to love God's will.
17. Fasting stirs the heart to seek the things that are above.
18. Fasting stirs people out of unholy inertia.
19. Fasting breaks the power of procrastination.
20. Fasting draws the fasting one nearer to God.
21. Fasting makes the presence of God nearer, clearer and swee-

ter.
22. Fasting brings hope and encouragement.
23. Fasting releases faith to believe that God will win in the coming battle.
24. Fasting makes it easier to forgive oneself.
25. Fasting renders the heart more open to restoration to God and man.
26. Fasting enlarges the heart to contain the purposes of God.
27. Fasting makes prayer more real.
28. Fasting intensifies prayer.
29. Fasting makes it easier to receive revelation from God's word.
30. Fasting makes it easier to discern God's voice.
31. Fasting liberates Spiritual power.
32. Fasting is a spiritual weapon that enhances the other spiritual weapons.
33. Fasting lays a claim on God to act, and He does act.
34. Fasting is an expression of spiritual desperation.
35. Fasting is a way of importuning God to act.
36. Fasting and prayer precipitate victory.
37. Fasting is a decision of the will.
38. Fasting people are closer to God.
39. Fasting people know God better.
40. Fasting people live longer.
41. Fasting people are more alert spiritually.
42. Fasting is a way of saying to God, " I will not let You go until You answer me. "
43. Fasting is a way of saying to God, " The issue before me is more important than food. "
44. The fall came because the fruit was eaten. Fasting is saying

" No " to the dominion of food.
45. Fasting opens a way to freedom from the power of food.
46. Fasting is a way of saying " No " to gluttony.

FASTING - 2

1. The quality of the fast is determined by the following :
2. Purity of heart.
3. Consecration to the Lord.
4. Love for the Lord.
5. Self-denial.
6. Suffering for the Lord.
7. Sacrifice for the Lord.
8. Knowledge of the Lord.
9. Extent of withdrawal into God's presence.
10. Quality of prayer during the fast.
11. Secrecy of the fast.
12. Hunger for God.
13. Obedience to the Lord.

FASTING - 3

The impact of a fast is directly proportional to the quality of the fast. The impact of the fast is also directly proportional to the duration of the fast. Everything being equal, for the same person a seven-day fast will produce results that cannot be produced by a three-day fast ; a three-week fast will produce results that cannot be produced by a seven-day fast. The Enemy asks, " Who is fasting ? " He is demanding to know the quality of the fast. The Enemy also asks, " For how long is he fasting ?" He is demanding to know the quantity of the fast . By these two factors , the Enemy will access what harm the fast will do on his kingdom.

So impact is directly proportional to the quality and quantity of the fast.

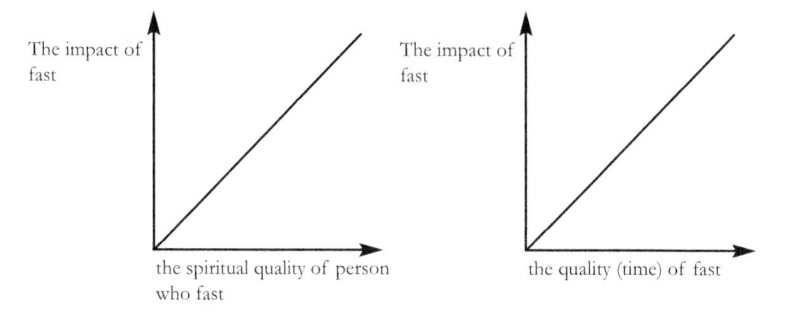

```
The impact of              The impact of
fast                       fast

      │  /                       │  /
      │ /                        │ /
      │/                         │/
      └──────────►               └──────────►
    the spiritual quality of person    the quality (time) of fast
    who fast
```

HANNAH FASTED

" *She wept and would not eat* " (1 Samuel 1 :7).

" *Then she went her way and ate something, and her face was no longer downcast* " (1 Samuel 1 :18).

Hannah was in bitterness of soul, wept much, fasted and prayed.

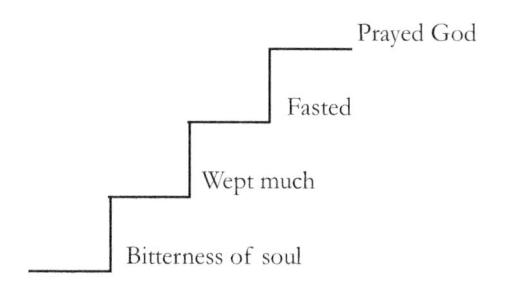

```
                              ┌──── Prayed God
                       ┌──── Fasted
                ┌──── Wept much
         ┌──── Bitterness of soul
```

Nehemiah said, "*When I heard these things, I sat down and wept. For some days I mourned and fasted and prayed before the God of heaven*" (Nehemiah 1:4).

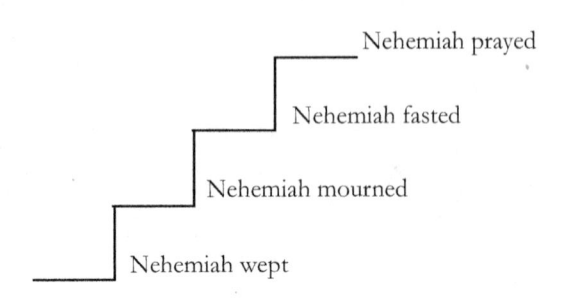

```
            ┌─── Nehemiah prayed
        ┌───┘ Nehemiah fasted
    ┌───┘ Nehemiah mourned
────┘ Nehemiah wept
```

Could the problem with the prayers of many people be the fact that they pray before they have wept, mourned and fasted? Could it be that unprepared people are attempting to do business at the throne of God? Might that explain the poor results from such careless praying?

It is most interesting that the Lord Jesus the Lord of all glory also walked along the same pathway. The Bible says, "*Then Jesus went with his disciples to a place called Gethsemane, and he said to them, 'Sit here while I go over there and pray.' He took Peter and the two sons of Zebedee along with him, and he began to be sorrowful and troubled. Then he said to them, 'My soul is overwhelmed with sorrow to the point of death. Stay here and keep watch with me.' Going a little further, he fell with his face to the ground and prayed, 'My Father, if it is possible, may this cup be taken from me. Yet not as I will, but as you will'*" (Matthew 26:36-39).

So for the Lord Jesus it was as follows :

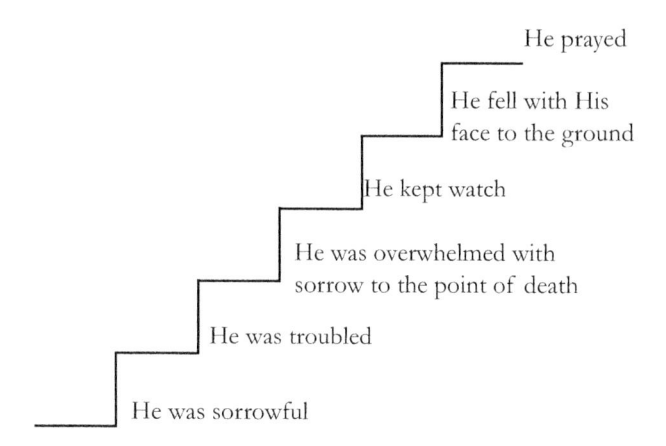

```
                                    He prayed
                        He fell with His
                        face to the ground
                    He kept watch
            He was overwhelmed with
            sorrow to the point of death
        He was troubled
    He was sorrowful
```

CHAPTER 13

THE BATTLE TO GIVE GOD A PROPHET FOR ISRAEL : HANNAH PRAYED TO THE LORD

As we saw in the last chapter, Hannah trod a certain pathway that led her to pray.

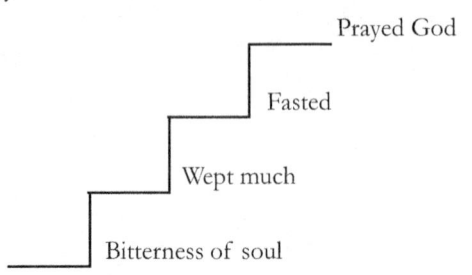

```
                          ┌──── Prayed God
                    ┌──── Fasted
              ┌──── Wept much
         ─────Bitterness of soul
```

Why was it necessary for her to walk along the pathway above before she prayed ? Why did Nehemiah walk the same pathway before he prayed ? Why did the Lord walk the same pathway ?

There are many reasons for this. One of the reasons is that listening ought to precede talking during prayer. A person ought to listen to God and only pray after God has spoken to him.

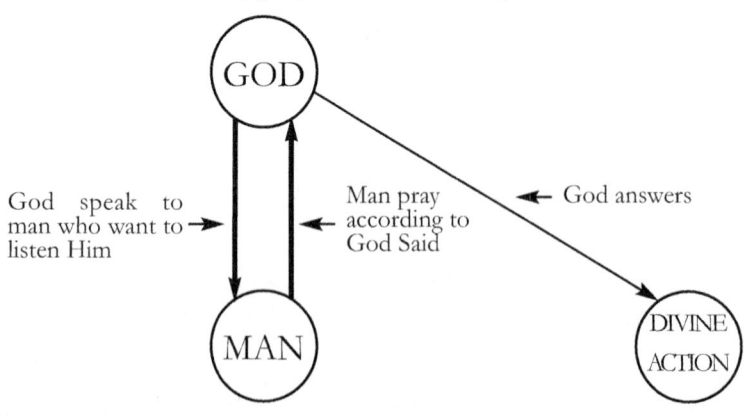

```
                    ( GOD )
                   ↑      ↓  ↖
God speak to       Man pray      ← God answers
man who want to →  ← according to
listen Him         God Said
                                        ( DIVINE
                    ( MAN )              ACTION )
```

The Bible says, "*Guard your steps when you go to the house of God. Go near to listen rather than to offer the sacrifice of fools, who do not know that they do wrong. Do not be quick with your mouth, do not be hasty in your heart to utter anything before God. God is in heaven and you are on earth, so let your words be few. As a dream comes when there are many cares, so the speech of a fool when there are many words"* (Ecclesiastes 5 :1-3).

   Prayer ought to begin in the heart of God !
   Prayer ought to be the discharge of a divine burden ! !
   Prayer ought to be the proclamation of the will of God ! ! !

Therefore a person ought to listen, hear God and then pray accordingly.

Another aspect of the matter is that we do not know what to ask God in prayer. The Bible says, " *In the same way, the Spirit helps us in our weakness. We do not know what we ought to pray for, but the Spirit himself intercedes for us with groans that words cannot express. And he who searches our hearts knows the mind of the Spirit, because the Spirit intercedes for the saints in accordance with God s will*" (Romans 8 :26-27).

If we do not know what we ought to pray for and yet we set out to pray, we may come to realize that we are not praying to God. Uttering that which is the will of the flesh, uttering that which originates in the flesh, uttering that which has as its goal the satisfaction of the flesh cannot be praying to God. All noise that is made by man in the name of prayer is not necessarily praying to God. Man can pray to himself. The Bible says, " *The Pharisee stood up and prayed to himself* " (Luke 18 :11).

Hannah prayed to God. She was carrying God's burden ; she was praying according to God's will.

However, it is possible that a person can carry a burden that is

God's and yet not pray to God. It is possible that a person can carry a burden that is God's and yet pray to himself. How is this possible ? This is possible because contact with God precedes praying to God. A person who is carrying a burden that is divine in origin must pluck in to God before he can pray to God. Unless he has plugged in to God, he can only make noise. He cannot pray to God.

What is involved in plugging in to God ? I think the best thing is to illustrate it from the life of Moses. The Bible says, " *The Lord said to Moses, ' Come up to me on the mountain and stay here, and I will give you the tablets of stone, with the law and commands I have written for their instruction. ' Then Moses set out with Joshua his aide, and Moses went up on the mountain of God... When Moses went up on the mountain, the cloud covered it, and the glory of the Lord settled on Mount Sinai. For six days the cloud covered the mountain, and on the seventh day the Lord called to Moses from within the cloud... Then Moses entered the cloud as he went on up the mountain. And he stayed on the mountain forty days and forty nights* " (Exodus 24 :12-18).

Moses needed six days to plug in to God. When he had plugged in, the Lord called to Moses in the cloud. God is always ready. If Moses had been ready after one day, God would have called him into the cloud. If he had been ready after three days, God would have called him. On the fifth day Moses was not yet ready. On the sixth day he was ready . As soon as he was ready, God called him into the cloud . As long as he was not ready God waited until he was ready.

The same thing happened with the Prophet Elijah. The Bible says, "*The Lord said, ' Go out and stand on the mountain in the presence of the Lord, for the Lord is about to pass by.' Then a great and powerful wind tore the mountains apart and shattered the rocks before the Lord, but the Lord was not in the wind. After the wind there was an earthquake, but the Lord was not in the earthquake. After the earthquake came a fire, but the Lord was not in the fire. And after the fire came a gentle whisper. When Elijah heard it, he pulled his cloak over his face and went out and stood at the mouth of the cave. Then a voice said to him, ' What are you doing here, Elijah ? '* " (1 Kings 19 :11-13).

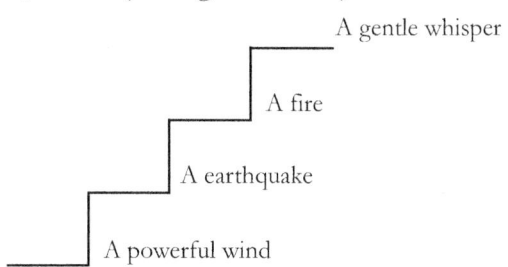

```
                          ┌──── A gentle whisper
                    ┌─────┘ A fire
              ┌─────┘ A earthquake
        ──────┘ A powerful wind
```

If Elijah had not been plugged in to God, he would have missed God's voice. He might have reasoned and said, " This powerful wind that has torn the mountains apart and shattered the rocks must be the voice of God ! " Or, he might have said, " Did the Lord not manifest Himself on Mount Carmel through the fire that fell on the sacrifice ? This must be the fire of God and consequently the voice of God ! " He was plugged in to God and so was not mistaken.

The last thing we want to say here about praying to God is that the time that it takes to plug in to God allows the person who wants to pray to sort out his motives. In the immediate presence of God we may see ourselves as we are, see our motives for what they are and, by the grace of God, see what God wants. When we thus see things we may discover that some things that we wanted to pray about are wrong and, therefore, should not be brought to God. We may also realize that some things that we thought we wanted God to give us are no longer necessary and, therefore, we should not ask Him. Finally, we may discover that the price that we would have to pay in order to co-operate with God to receive the answer to our request is beyond what we want to pay and so refuse to take the matter with God. This will do us good.

Hannah went through the test of bitterness of soul, much weeping and fasting, and was ready. She then prayed to God. She was sure about her request. She was plugged in to God. She prayed to God !

Hallelujah !

May the Lord enable each one of us to follow her example !

Amen.

CHAPTER 14

THE BATTLE TO GIVE GOD A PROPHET FOR ISRAEL :
HANNAH'S REQUEST

We saw in the last chapter that Hannah prayed to God. It will be good to look at what she said to God. The Bible says, "*And she made a vow, saying, 'O Lord Almighty, if you will only look upon your servant's misery and remember me, and not forget your servant but give her a son, then I will give him to the Lord for all the days of his life, and no razor will ever be used on his head*'" (1 Samuel 1:11).

PRAYER : ASKING AND RECEIVING FROM GOD

Sometimes people make a lot of noise and it does not seem to be clear what they are asking God to do. This is confusion. Let us look at some prayers of the Bible to strengthen what we are saying.

The Bible says, "*When David learned that Saul was plotting against him, he said to Abiathar the priest, 'Bring the ephod.' David said, 'O Lord, God of Israel, your servant has heard definitely that Saul plans to come to Keilah and destroy the town on account of me. Will the citizens of Keilah surrender me to him? Will Saul come down, as your servant has heard? O Lord, God of Israel, tell your servant.' And the Lord said, 'He will.' Again David asked, 'Will the citizens of Keilah surrender me and my men to Saul?' And the Lord said, 'They will.' So David and his men, about six hundred in number, left Keilah and kept moving from place to place. When Saul was told that David had escaped from Keilah, he did not go there*" (1 Samuel 23:9-13).

David knew what he wanted. He wanted information from the Lord so as to know what to do in order to escape from Saul. He asked clearly. We can set forth his requests and the answers he received as follows :

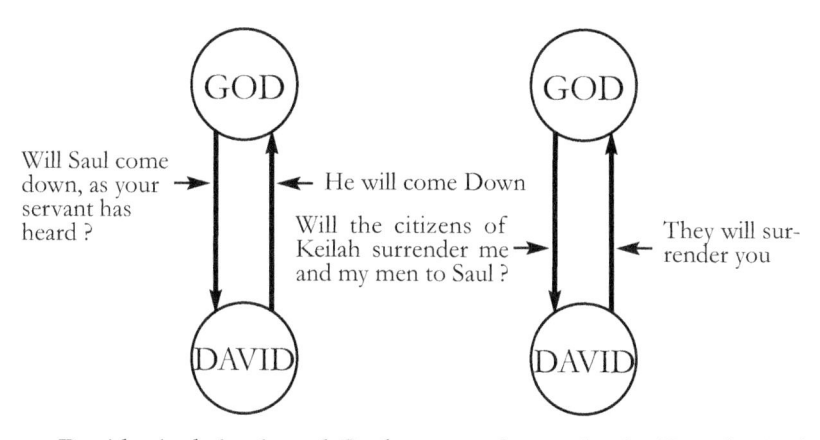

```
        GOD                          GOD
         ↑↓                           ↑↓
Will Saul come                                    
down, as your  →  ← He will come Down
servant has
heard ?        Will the citizens of     They will sur-
               Keilah surrender me →  ← render you
               and my men to Saul ?
        DAVID                        DAVID
```

David asked clearly and God answered very clearly. David asked and supplicated a bit. After asking he added, " O Lord God of Israel, tell your servant. " Even if he had not supplicated, he would still have prayed. All was clear and he received clear answers.

The Bible again says, " *When he came down from the mountainside, large crowds followed him. A man with leprosy came and knelt before him and said, ' Lord, if you are willing, you can make me clean.' Jesus reached out his hand and touched the man. 'I am willing,' he said. 'Be clean !' Immediately he was cured of his leprosy* " (Matthew 8 :1-3). We again present it as follows :

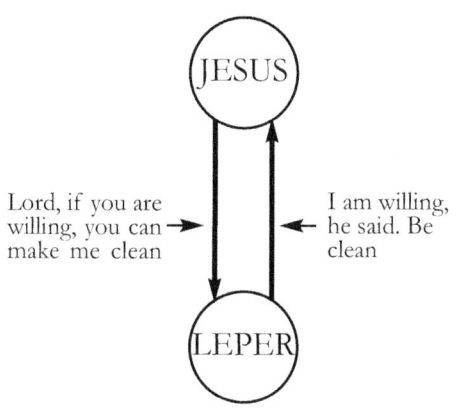

```
              JESUS
               ↑↓
Lord, if you are          I am willing,
willing, you can  →   ←   he said. Be
make me clean             clean
              LEPER
```

The leper asked clearly and simply, and the Lord gave him what he asked for.

Saul of Tarsus asked, " *Who are you, Lord ?* " The Lord Jesus answered, " *I am Jesus, whom you are persecuting* " (Acts 9 :5).

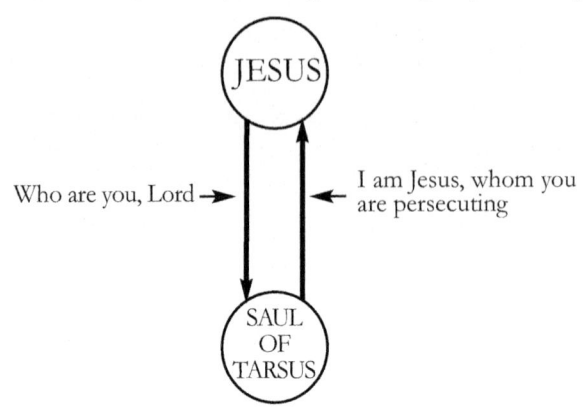

ASKING CLEARLY

Many people do not pray because they do not know what to ask. Others have things to ask, but they say so many things that what they are asking becomes confused. If a person does not know very clearly what he wants from God, how can he ask ? If it is not clear in his mind, how can he expect an answer ? If it is not clear in his mind what he wants God to do for him, how can he exercise faith for answers ? To ask clearly is of utmost importance in prayer.

I record my prayer requests in tabular form as shown below. This helps me to be specific. This helps me also to press on until answers come.

N°	DATE FIRST PRAYED	TOPIC OF PRAYER	BIBLE BACKING	DATE ANSWERED	HOW ANSWERED
1	10.08.97	Lord, save Simon Awanchiri.	2 Pet 3:9		
2	10.08.97	Lord, save Joshua Gwan.	2 Pet. 3:9		
3	10.08.97	Lord, give us Elizabeth's first term fees.	Phil. 4:19		
4	10.08.97	Lord, give us Stephen's first semester fees.	Phil. 4:19		
5	10.08.97	Lord, heal the eyes of Stacey Aldred.	1 Pet. 2:24		
6	10.08.97	Lord, what do you want me to do in India in 1998 ?	Psalm 32:8		
7	10.08.97	Lord, what subjects should John Fomum do in High School ?	Psalm 32:8		
8	10.08.97	Lord, give us a missionary couple for South Africa.	Mark 16:15		
9	10.08.97	Lord, give a visa for our missionary couple for Australia.	Mark 16:15		
10	10.08.97	Lord, enable us to start the Yaounde Orphanage.	John 15:5		
11	10.08.97	Lord, enable me to complete the Missionary studio.	Phil. 4:19		
12	10.08.97	Lord, provide an office for Mrs Prisca Fomum.	Phil. 4:6		
13	10.08.97	Lord, give me another vision of heaven.	John 16:13		
14	10.08.97	Lord, give me another vision of hell.	John 10:13		
15	10.08.97	Lord, give our ministry registration with the Indian government.	Ezra 1:1		
16	10.08.97	Lord, open a door for me to preach Christ in Pakistan.	Rev. 3:8		
17	10.08.97	Lord, enable Elizabeth to complete the 21 day fast of September	Isaiah 40:31		
18	10.08.97	Lord, add the next 1000 people to the Church in Yaounde.	Acts 2:47		

A person must ask himself, " When the answer to my prayer request comes", will I be able to recognize it ? If the answer is "Yes ", then his request is most likely specific.

HANNAH'S REQUEST

To simply ask clearly, Hannah could have said to God, " Lord, give me a son, " and that would have been enough. However, she did not only ask clearly. She supplicated ! What was at stake was such that she had to do everything that she knew how to, in order to move God to answer her.

CHAPTER 15

THE BATTLE TO GIVE GOD A PROPHET FOR ISRAEL: THE MINISTRY OF SUPPLICATION

WHAT IS SUPPLICATION

Supplication is humble, earnest entreating of God in prayer. It is humbly doing all that can be done to move God to grant a request. It is humbly begging God to provide a solution.

With that definition we can now look at the prayer of Hannah to see what she said to supplicate God. First of all, she made a vow to God. Secondly, she kept on praying to the Lord. Thirdly, she prayed out of deep trouble. Fourthly, she poured out her soul to the Lord. Fifthly, she prayed out of her great anguish and grief. These five additions to her prayer were her supplication.

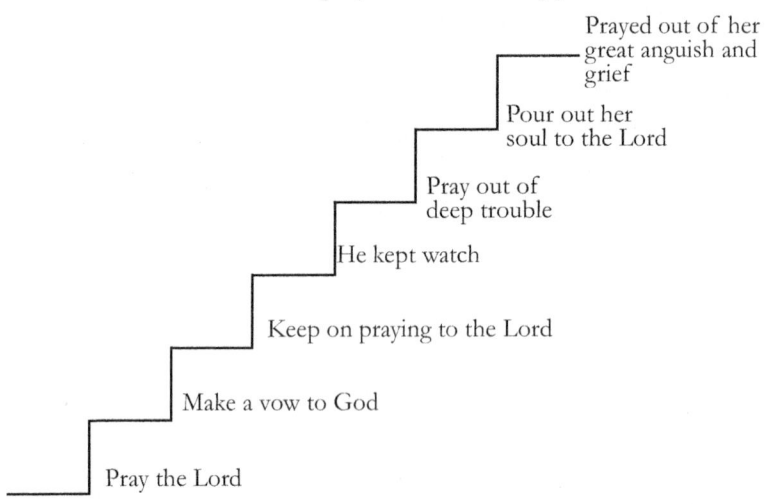

- Prayed out of her great anguish and grief
- Pour out her soul to the Lord
- Pray out of deep trouble
- He kept watch
- Keep on praying to the Lord
- Make a vow to God
- Pray the Lord

There was bitterness of soul, weeping and fasting to prepare to gain access into the presence of God. When that access was gained, she prayed. That could have brought things to an end were she not supplicating. We can then say that supplication is what a person " does " in addition to simply praying when the person has plugged in, tuned in, entered into contact with God. Supplication is what a person does, not only to present a request to the Lord, but to ensure that the Lord hears him and answers him.

Could the reason why many believers do not receive God's answers to some of their prayers be owing to the fact that they stop at simple asking, whereas the issue about which they are praying requires supplication to get through ?

Moses went back to the mountain to intercede for Israel. The Bible says, " I lay prostrate before the Lord those forty days and forty nights because the Lord had said he would destroy you. I prayed to the Lord and said, ' O Sovereign Lord, do not destroy your people, your own inheritance that you redeemed by your great power and brought out of Egypt with a mighty hand. Remember your servants Abraham, Isaac and Jacob. Overlook the stubbornness of this people, their wickedness and their sin. Otherwise, the country from which you brought us will say, " *Because the Lord was not able to take them into the land he had promised them, and because he hated them, he brought them out to put them to death in the desert. But they are your people, your inheritance that you brought out by your great power and your outstretched arm* " (Deuteronomy 9 :25-29).

If Moses had simply prayed, saying, " O Sovereign Lord, do not destroy your people, " it would still have been intercession. However, he did not only intercede. He supplicated as he interceded. This went on for forty days and nights. Then he came to the place of victory. If he had not pressed on to the end, he would have failed to obtain what he desired.

The supplicant leaves no stone unturned to ensure that God grants his request. Nehemiah supplicated. He prayed, saying to the Lord, " *O Lord, God of heaven, the great and awesome God, who keeps his covenant of love with those who love him and obey his commands, let your ear be attentive and your eyes open to hear the prayer your servant is praying before you day and night for your servants, the people of Israel. I confess the sins we Israelites, including myself and my father's house, have committed against you. We have acted very wickedly towards you. We have not obeyed the commands, decrees and laws you gave your servant Moses.*

Remember the instruction you gave your servant Moses, saying, If you are unfaithful, I will scatter you among the nations, but if you return to me and obey my commands, then even if your exiled people are at the farthest horizon, I will gather them from there and bring them to the place I have chosen as a dwelling for my name.

They are your servants and your people, whom you redeemed by your great strength and your mighty hand. O Lord, let your ear be attentive to the prayer of this your servant and to the prayer of your servants who delight in revering your name. Give your servant success today by granting him favour in the presence of this man" (Nehemiah 1:5-11).

If Nehemiah had wanted to ask simply, he could just have prayed, " Give your servant success today by granting him favour in the presence of this man." This was the core request. The rest was

- the supplication
- the pleading
- the beseeching
- the begging
- the moving

of God to answer!

He laboured to supplicate so much because he could not afford not to be heard. So much was at stake! Supplication is the labour before God in prayer by a person who cannot accept a " No " from

God for an answer !

Do you have any issues to pray about for which you must have God answer in the affirmative ? Such issues will compel you to supplicate. Those who can go unheard do not need to supplicate. They can continue even if God does not answer their prayer. They have nothing at stake and often God lets them go unheard ; for God does not delight to trouble people with answers. He moves when He has been moved to move. He moves when He must move.

Dare to move God to move !

Dare to press on for His answer ! !

CHAPTER 16

THE BATTLE TO GIVE GOD A PROPHET FOR ISRAEL : HANNAH'S SUPPLICATION THROUGH A VOW

HANNAH'S VOW

Hannah, in making her request, said to God, " If you give me a son, I will give that son to you all the days of his life. " She was saying to God, " God, give me a son and I will ensure that that son serves Your purposes all his life." This was another way of supplicating. She was supplicating by labouring to show God the fact that God's purposes would be advanced if He answered her prayer. She was going out of her way to let God know that her request was God-centred and not self-centred. She vowed to prove to God her earnestness in this matter. She vowed to move God to act in her favour. She vowed to convince God that she could be depended upon. The vow was all a part of her labour to move God to act.

VOWS ARE BINDING - 1

The Bible says the following about vows : " *Moses said to the heads of the tribes of Israel : ' This is what the Lord commands : When a man makes a vow to the Lord or takes an oath to bind himself by a pledge , he must not break his word but must do everything he said. ' When a young woman still living in her father's house makes a vow to the Lord or binds herself by a pledge and her father hears about her vow or pledge but says nothing to her, then all her vows and every pledge by which she bound herself will stand. But if her father forbids her when he hears about it, none of her vows or the pledges by which she bound herself will stand ; the Lord will release her because her father has forbidden her.*

If she marries after she makes a vow or after her lips utter a rash promise by which she binds herself and her husband hears about it but says nothing to her, then her vows or the pledges by which she bound herself will stand. But if her husband forbids her when he hears about it, he nullifies the vow that binds her or the rash promise by which she binds herself, and the Lord will release her. Any vow or obligation taken by a widow or divorced woman will be binding on her ' " (Numbers 30 :1-9).

Vows are binding !

VOWS ARE BINDING - 2

The Bible says, " *Now when all the kings west of the Jordan heard about these things - those in the hill country, in the western foothills, and along the entire coast of the Great Sea as far as Lebanon...... they came together to make war against Joshua and Israel.*

However, when the people of Gibeon heard what Joshua had done to Jericho and Ai, they resorted to a ruse.... The men of Israel sampled their provisions but did not enquire of the Lord. Then Joshua made a treaty of peace with them to let them live, and the leaders of the assembly ratified it by oath.

Three days after they made the treaty with the Gibeonites, the Israelites heard that they were neighbours, living near them. So the Israelites set out and on the third day came to their cities : Gibeon, Kephirah, Beeroth and Kiriath Jearim. But the Israelites did not attack them, because the leaders of the assembly had sworn an oath to them by the Lord, the God of Israel.

The whole assembly grumbled against the leaders, but all the leaders answered, ' We have given them our oath by the Lord, the God of Israel, and we cannot touch them now. This is what we will do to them : We will let them live, so that wrath will not fall on us for breaking the oath we swore to them " (Joshua 9 :1-20).

VOWS ARE BINDING - 3

"*Then the Spirit of the Lord came upon Jephthah. He crossed Gilead and Manasseh, passed through Mizpah of Gilead, and from there he advanced against the Ammonites. And <u>Jephthah made a vow to the Lord : 'If you give the Ammonites into my hands, whatever comes out of the door of my house to meet me when I return in triumph from the Ammonites will be the Lord's , and I will sacrifice it as a burnt offering</u>.*'

Then Jephthah went over to fight the Ammonites, and the Lord gave them into his hands. He devastated twenty towns from Aroer to the vicinity of Minnith, as far as Abel Keramim. Thus Israel subdued Ammon.

<u>When Jephthah returned to his home in Mizpah, who should come out to meet him but his daughter, dancing to the sound of tambourines ! She was an only child. Except for her he had neither son nor daughter. When he saw her, he tore his clothes and cried, ' Oh ! my daughter ! You have made me miserable and wretched, because I have made a vow to the Lord that I cannot break.</u>

<u>' My father, ' she replied, ' you have given your word to the Lord. Do to me just as you promised, now that the Lord has avenged you of your enemies, the Ammonites.</u> But grant me this one request, ' she said. ' Give me two months to roam the hills and weep with my friends, because I will never marry.

' You may go, ' he said. And he let her go for two months. She and the girls went into the hills and wept because she would never marry. After the two months, she returned to her father and <u>he did to her as he had vowed</u>. And she was a virgin " (Judges 11 :29-39).

VOWS ARE BINDING- 4

"Lord, who may dwell in your sanctuary ?
Who may live on your holy hill ?
He whose walk is blameless
and who does what is righteous,
who speaks the truth from his heart
and has no slander on his tongue,
who does his neighbour no wrong
and casts no slur on his fellow-man,
who despises a vile man

*but honours those who fear the Lord,
<u>who keeps his oath even when it hurts</u>*" (Psalm 15:1-4).

*" Sacrifice thank-offerings to God,
<u>fulfil your vows to the Most High</u>,
and call upon me in the day of trouble ;
I will deliver you, and you will honour me "* (Psalm 50:14-15).

*"<u>I am under vows to you, O God</u> ;
I will present my thank-offerings to you"* (Psalm 56:12).

*"For you have heard my vows, O God.....
Then will I ever sing praise to your name
and fulfil my vows day after day"* (Psalm 61:5-8).

*"Praise awaits you, O God, in Zion ;
to you our vows will be fulfilled.
O you who hear prayer, to you all men will come"* (Psalm 65:1-2).

*"I will come to your temple with burnt offerings
and fulfil my vows to you
vows my lips promised and my mouth spoke
when I was in trouble"* (Psalm 66:13-14).

VOWS ARE BINDING - 5

"When you make a vow to God, do not delay in fulfilling it. He has no pleasure in fools ; fulfil your vow. It is better not to vow than to make a vow and not fulfil it. Do not let your mouth lead you into sin. And do not protest to the temple messenger, 'My vow was a mistake.' Why should God be angry at what you say and destroy the work of your hands ? Much

dreaming and many words are meaningless. Therefore stand in awe of God" (Ecclesiastes 5 :4-7).

"As for younger widows, do not put them on such a list. For when their sensual desires overcome their dedication to Christ, they want to marry. Thus they bring judgment on themselves, because they have broken their first pledge" (1 Timothy 5 :11-12).

THE BELIEVER'S WORDS ARE BINDING

" Again, you have heard that it was said to the people long ago, 'Do not break your oath, but keep the oaths you have made to the Lord.' But I tell you, Do not swear at all : either by heaven, for it is God's throne ; or by the earth, for it is his footstool ; or by Jerusalem, for it is the city of the Great King. And do not swear by your head, for you cannot make even one hair white or black. Simply let your 'Yes' be 'Yes' and your 'No', 'No', anything beyond this comes from the evil one" (Matthew 5 :33-37).

When a believer in Christ says : " Yes " or " No " he has committed himself by thus saying and must live in such a way that that " Yes " always remains " Yes " and that " No " always remains " No ". The word of a believer is at least as binding as a vow. This means that

- every word
- commitment
- covenant
- engagement

of a believer is absolutely binding. When a believer speaks, he has spoken. He has committed himself irrevocably.

COMMITMENTS AND PRAYER

Hannah vowed and it was understood that she would keep her

vow at any cost to herself. If a man makes promises to God and does not keep them, when he prays God will not hear him. When a man makes commitments to God and changes his mind and does not fulfil what he had said to God, when he makes requests, God will consider them as things about which he will soon change his mind. Consequently, God will not take his prayers seriously. God will not answer them.

Only people who match their commitments with their deeds are taken seriously by God. Only they can pray and be heard. The Bible says, *"No-one who practises deceit will dwell in my house ; no-one who speaks falsely will stand in my presence"* (Psalm 101 :7).

TO COMMIT OR NOT TO COMMIT ONESELF

There are three types of people. There are those who make no covenants ; there are those who make covenants and break them and there are those who make covenants and keep them. Those who make covenants and keep them make the most progress, since they labour to keep the covenants and in so labouring make progress. There are those who make no covenants and, lastly, there are those who make covenants and break them.

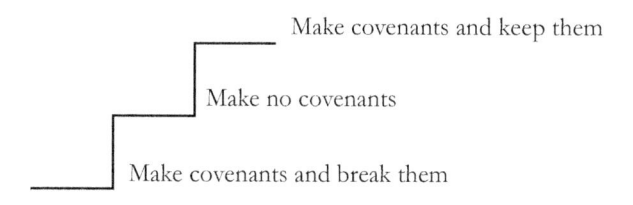

```
          _____ Make covenants and keep them
         |
         |____ Make no covenants
              |
         _____| Make covenants and break them
```

OUR GOD : A COVENANT-KEEPING GOD

The Bible says, " *The angel of the Lord called to Abraham from heaven a second time and said, 'I swear by myself,' declares the Lord, 'that because you have done this and have not withheld your son, your only son, I will surely bless you and make your descendants as numerous as the stars in the sky and as the sand on the seashore. Your descendants will take possession of the cities of their enemies, and through your offspring all nations on earth will be blessed, because you have obeyed me '"* (Genesis 22 :15-18).

Again the Bible says, " *When God made his promise to Abraham, since there was no-one greater for him to swear by, he swore by himself, saying, 'I will surely bless you and give you many descendants.' And so after waiting patiently, Abraham received what was promised. Men swear by someone greater than themselves, and the oath confirms what is said and puts an end to all argument. Because God wanted to make the unchanging nature of his purpose very clear to the heirs of what was promised, he confirmed it with an oath. God did this so that, by two unchangeable things in which it is impossible for God to lie, we who have fled to take hold of the hope offered to us may be greatly encouraged* " (Hebrews 6 :13-18).

THE AUTHOR'S COMMITMENTS TO GOD

I, the author, like Hannah have made commitments to God. They are as follows:

1. I make God: the Father, the Son and the Holy Spirit my supreme Love, my supreme Joy and my supreme Bliss.
2. I make the winning of the lost to Christ and the perfection of His Bride-elect the supreme compulsion of my life.
3. I make the world, the devil and the flesh my fiercest foes.
4. I will labour, the Holy Spirit being my Helper, to be the slave of the Lord Jesus Christ in everything and at all times.

5. I will labour, the Holy Spirit being my Helper, to be the slave of my wife in everything and at all times.
6. I will labour, the Holy Spirit being my Helper, to be the slave of my children in everything and at all times.
7. I will labour, the Holy Spirit being my Helper, to be the slave of my driver in everything and at all times.
8. I will labour, the Holy Spirit being my Helper, to be the slave of my secretary in everything and at all times.
9. I will labour, the Holy Spirit being my Helper, to be the slave of my other co-workers in everything and at all times.
10. I will labour, the Holy Spirit being my Helper, to be the slave of the elders in the church in Yaounde in everything and at all times.
11. I will labour, the Holy Spirit being my Helper, to be the slave of every member of the church in Yaounde in everything and at all times.
12. I will labour, the Holy Spirit being my Helper, to be the slave of every believer in Yaounde in everything and at all times.
13. I will labour, the Holy Spirit being my Helper, to be the slave of every believer in Cameroon in everything and at all times.
14. I will labour, the Holy Spirit being my Helper, to be the slave of every believer in Africa in everything and at all times.
15. I will labour, the Holy Spirit being my Helper, to be the slave of every believer on Planet Earth in everything and at all times.
16. I will labour, the Holy Spirit being my Helper, to be the slave of everyone in authority over me in everything and at all times.
17. I will labour, the Holy Spirit being my Helper, to be the slave of my Head of Department in everything and at all times.
18. I will labour, the Holy Spirit being my Helper, to be the slave of my colleagues in everything and at all times.
19. I will labour, the Holy Spirit being my Helper, to be the slave of my students in everything and at all times.

20. I will labour, the Holy Spirit being my Helper, to be the slave of every worker in the University of Yaounde in everything and at all times.
21. I will labour, the Holy Spirit being my Helper, to be the slave of every human being in Yaounde in everything and at all times.
22. I will labour, the Holy Spirit being my Helper, to be the slave of every human being in Cameroon in everything and at all times.
23. I will labour, the Holy Spirit being my Helper, to be the slave of every human being in Africa in everything and at all times.
24. I will labour, the Holy Spirit being my Helper, to be the slave of every human being on the Planet Earth in everything and at all times.
25. I gladly accept to be blamed because of the Lord Jesus and the Gospel.
26. I gladly accept to be dishonoured because of the Lord Jesus and the Gospel.
27. I gladly accept to be ill-spoken of because of the Lord Jesus and the Gospel.
28. I gladly accept to be undesired because of the Lord Jesus and the Gospel.
29. I gladly accept to be ignored because of the Lord Jesus and the Gospel.
30. I gladly accept to be treated with contempt because of the Lord Jesus and the Gospel.
31. I gladly accept to be neglected because of the Lord Jesus and the Gospel.
32. I gladly accept to be forgotten because of the Lord Jesus and the Gospel.
33. I gladly accept to be considered a failure by the world because of the Lord Jesus and the Gospel.
34. I gladly accept to be cited by unbelievers as a failure because of

the Lord Jesus and the Gospel.

35. I gladly accept to be hated because of the Lord Jesus and the Gospel.
36. I gladly accept to be disapproved because of the Lord Jesus and the Gospel.
37. I gladly accept to be contradicted because of the Lord Jesus and the Gospel.
38. I gladly accept to be cheated because of the Lord Jesus and the Gospel.
39. I gladly accept to be abused because of the Lord Jesus and the Gospel.
40. I gladly accept to be insulted because of the Lord Jesus and the Gospel.
41. I gladly accept to serve because of the Lord Jesus and the Gospel.
42. I gladly accept to be the last because of the Lord Jesus and the Gospel.
43. I gladly accept to be demoted because of the Lord Jesus and the Gospel.
44. I gladly accept to be dependent on man because of the Lord Jesus and the Gospel.
45. I gladly accept to be under authority because of the Lord Jesus and the Gospel.
46. I gladly accept to be commanded because of the Lord Jesus and the Gospel.
47. I gladly accept to be rebuked because of the Lord Jesus and the Gospel.
48. I gladly accept to be ridiculed because of the Lord Jesus and the Gospel.
49. I gladly accept to be scandalized because of the Lord Jesus and the Gospel.

50. I gladly accept to be made as uncomfortable as possible because of the Lord Jesus and the Gospel.
51. I gladly accept to be deprived of my rights because of the Lord Jesus and the Gospel.
52. I gladly accept to be deprived of my privileges because of the Lord Jesus and the Gospel.
53. I gladly accept to be disgraced because of the Lord Jesus and the Gospel.
54. I gladly accept to be made ashamed because of the Lord Jesus and the Gospel.
55. I gladly accept to be reproached because of the Lord Jesus and the Gospel.
56. I commit myself, the Lord being my Helper, never to desire to be seen.
57. I commit myself, the Lord being my Helper, never to desire to be heard.
58. I commit myself, the Lord being my Helper, never to desire to be appreciated.
59. I commit myself, the Lord being my Helper, never to desire to be approved.
60. I commit myself, the Lord being my Helper, never to desire to be honoured.
61. I commit myself, the Lord being my Helper, never to desire to be first before man.
62. I commit myself, the Lord being my Helper, never to desire to be praised.
63. I commit myself, the Lord being my Helper, never to desire to be served.
64. I commit myself, the Lord being my Helper, never to desire to be exalted.
65. I commit myself, the Lord being my Helper, never to desire to

be well-spoken of.
66. I commit myself, the Lord being my Helper, never to desire to be loved.
67. I commit myself, the Lord being my Helper, never to desire to be desired.
68. I commit myself, the Lord being my Helper, never to desire to be admired.
69. I commit myself, the Lord being my Helper, never to desire to be consulted.
70. I commit myself, the Lord being my Helper, never to desire to be pleased.
71. I commit myself, the Lord being my Helper, never to desire to be entertained.
72. I commit myself, the Lord being my Helper, never to desire to be remembered.
73. I commit myself, the Lord being my Helper, never to desire to be congratulated.
74. I commit myself, the Lord being my Helper, never to desire to be cited as a model.
75. I commit myself, the Lord being my Helper, never to desire to be obeyed.
76. I commit myself, the Lord being my Helper, never to desire to be known.
77. I commit myself, the Lord being my Helper, never to desire to be independent of man.
78. I commit myself, the Lord being my Helper, never to desire to be self-dependent.
79. I commit myself, the Lord being my Helper, never to desire to be self-sufficient.
80. I commit myself, the Lord being my Helper, never to desire to be in authority.

81. I commit myself, the Lord being my Helper, never to desire to be in command.
82. I commit myself, the Lord being my Helper, never to give anyone up, regardless of what he or she may do to me or to our ministry.
83. I will labour, the Lord being my Helper, to mature in love.
84. I will labour, the Lord being my Helper, to mature in joy.
85. I will labour, the Lord being my Helper, to mature in peace.
86. I will labour, the Lord being my Helper, to mature in patience.
87. I will labour, the Lord being my Helper, to mature in kindness.
88. I will labour, the Lord being my Helper, to mature in goodness.
89. I will labour, the Lord being my Helper, to mature in faithfulness.
90. I will labour, the Lord being my Helper, to mature in gentleness.
91. I will labour, the Lord being my Helper, to mature in self-control.
92. I commit myself, the Lord being my Helper, not to keep anything that I do not immediately need while someone else needs it at the moment.
93. I will fast for 36 hours every year as a Fasting Intercessor for Zacharias Fomum (FIFOZAFO).
94. I will fast for 48 hours every year as a Fasting Intercessor for the Zacharias Fomum family (FIFOZAFOFA).
95. I will fast for 72 hours every year as a Fasting Intercessor for Etoug-Ebe (FIFE).
96. I will fast for 96 hours every year as a Fasting Intercessor for Yaounde (FIFOCAM).
97. I will fast for 120 hours every year as a Fasting Intercessor for Cameroon (FIFOCAM).
98. I will fast for 144 hours every year as a Fasting Intercessor for

Africa (FIFA).
99. I will fast for 168 hours every year as a Fasting Intercessor for the Planet Earth (FIFOPE).
100. I will carry out three long fasts each year.
101. I will move God and man through fasting.
102. I will cut my body weight to 55-65 kilograms as the Lord asked of me.
103. I will constantly be absolutely pure in desire.
104. I will constantly be absolutely pure in thought.
105. I will constantly be absolutely pure in look.
106. I will constantly be absolutely pure in touch.
107. I will constantly be absolutely pure in word.
108. I will constantly be absolutely pure in deed.
109. I will live constantly in the immediate presence of the Lord.
110. I will labour to be welded increasingly to the Lord Jesus.
111. I will not allow any cloud to come between the Lord Jesus and myself.
112. I will die to self in every situation.
113. I will labour to know the Cross experientially in increasing depths.
114. I will ensure that I enter increasingly into the "Reproach of the Cross."
115. I will not allow any cloud between any human being and myself, as far as it depends on me.
116. I will not buy anything for myself that the Lord Jesus would not have bought for Himself.
117. I will not desire anything for myself that the Lord Jesus would not desire for Himself.
118. I will not have any thoughts that the Lord Jesus would not have.
119. I will not have any motive that the Lord Jesus would not have.

120. I will not give a second look to anything or anyone that the Lord Jesus would not give a second look to .
121. I will not have any tastes which the Lord Jesus would not have.
122. I will not have any feelings that the Lord Jesus would not have.
123. I will not touch anything or anyone that the Lord Jesus would not touch.
124. I will not say anything that the Lord Jesus would not say.
125. I will not do anything that the Lord Jesus would not do.
126. I will not make any plans that the Lord Jesus would not make.
127. I will invest all I have and all I can to seek the Lord desperately.
128. I will invest all I have and all I can to know the Lord as fully as it is possible.
129. I will labour, the Lord being my Helper, to ensure that all the glory for what I am and will ever be, for what I do and will ever do, for what I have and will ever have, is given exclusively to the Lord Jesus Christ.
130. I will labour to ensure that prayer precedes everything I do.
131. I will labour to ensure that I offer praise and thanksgiving to the Lord God Almighty for everything and at all times.
132. I will love every human being.
133. I will be the custodian of the wealth and possession of everyone on the Planet Earth.
134. I will not murmur.
135. I will not grumble.
136. I will not gossip.
137. I will not expose the fault of anyone to another.
138. I will not listen to gossip.
139. I will not slander anyone.
140. I will be the custodian of the reputation of every human being on the Planet Earth.

141. I will treat every human being as if he were me.
142. I will treat every human being as if he were the Lord Jesus.
143. I will be true in everything I think, say or do.
144. I will labour to make meekness and humility my way of life.
145. I take responsibility for all that may go wrong in my life, and commit myself not to blame anyone else for it.
146. I take responsibility for all that may go wrong in my family, and commit myself not to blame anyone else for it.
147. I take responsibility for all that may go wrong in the work that God has given us in Yaounde, and commit myself not to blame anyone else for it.
148. I take responsibility for all that may go wrong in the work that God has given us in Cameroon, and commit myself not to blame anyone else for it.
149. I take responsibility for all that may go wrong in the work that God has given us in Africa, and commit myself not to blame anyone else for it.
150. I take responsibility for all that may go wrong in the work that God has given us in Europe, and commit myself not to blame anyone else for it.
151. I take responsibility for all that may go wrong in the work that God has given us in Asia, and commit myself not to blame anyone else for it.
152. I take responsibility for all that may go wrong in the work that God has given us in North America, and commit myself not to blame anyone else for it.
153. I take responsibility for all that may go wrong in the work that God has given us in South America, and commit myself not to blame anyone else for it.
154. I take responsibility for all that may go wrong in the work that God has given us in Oceania, and commit myself not to blame

anyone else for it.

155. I gladly commit myself, the Lord being my Helper, to live in voluntary simplicity as far as the things of this world are concerned, so that the money that could have been invested on a luxurious life-style should be invested into the battle to reach out to the maximum number of lost people with the glorious Gospel.

156. I will have the minimum number of suits possible, so that the money that would have been spent on additional suits be invested into the battle to reach out to the maximum number of perishing souls with the glorious Gospel.

157. I will have the minimum number of jackets possible because of the perishing souls of men.

158. I will have the minimum number of pairs of shoes possible because of the perishing souls of men.

159. I will have the minimum number of shirts possible because of the perishing souls of men.

160. I will have the minimum number of trousers possible because of the perishing souls of men.

161. I will move the saints by prayer and fasting to invest in the Bank of Heaven.

162. I commit myself, the Lord being my Helper, not to advertise the financial needs of the work God has given us to do for Him but to move people by prayer and fasting to invest funds into the work.

163. I commit myself, the Lord being my Helper, not to ask anyone to make a sacrifice for our ministry which I am not already making or which I would not gladly make were I called to play his or her role.

164. I will be transparent in all I think, say or do.

165. I will not carry out any act that I would not want written across the sky for all to see.

166. I will not carry out any act that I would not want the whole world to do as I have done.
167. I separate myself from the burying of the dead. I will give myself to the living.
168. I will labour to ensure that I carry out each year three 40 day prayer crusades of 400 hours of praying per crusade.
169. I will labour to ensure that I carry out twelve prayer sieges every year.
170. I will labour to ensure that I carry out twelve writing crusades each year.
171. I will labour to ensure that I have three Bible reading crusades each year.
172. I will labour to ensure that I pray for an average of eight hours each day.
173. Prisca and I will labour to ensure that we pray together for eight hours in one go once each month, so as to build ourselves, our children and our household before God in prayer.
174. I separate myself from every negative thought, word and deed.
175. I will think, speak and act positively.
176. I will labour to ensure that I minister Christ in the six continents of the Planet Earth annually.
177. I will labour to ensure that I minister Christ in 25 countries each year.
178. I will labour to ensure that I minister Christ in 25 localities in Cameroon annually.
179. I will labour to write twelve Christian books each year.
180. I will labour to read 12 Christian books each year.
181. I will labour to ensure that I study 12 books each year.
182. I will invest my all not to be late or negligent with time in any way.

183. I separate myself from all politics permanently.
184. I will labour to ensure that I invest my all into the battle to reach everyone in Yaounde with the Gospel.
185. I will labour to ensure that I invest my all into the battle to reach everyone in Cameroon with the Gospel.
186. I will labour to ensure that I invest my all into the battle to reach everyone in Africa with the Gospel.
187. I will labour to ensure that I invest my all into the battle to reach everyone on the Planet Earth with the Gospel.
188. I will do all to accountably invest eighteen hours every day into God-approved projects.
189. I commit myself to read the Bible every day unfailingly.
190. I commit myself to read the Bible three times each year.
191. I commit myself to memorize fifty Bible verses each year.
192. I commit myself to have a dynamic encounter with the Lord every day.
193. I will seek, know and do God's will in everything.
194. I will never complain that I have no money.
195. I will prove by every form of answered prayer that God answers prayer.
196. I will move God and man through prayer.
197. I will labour to ensure that a major and continuous revival comes upon the people in our ministry.
198. I will do everything I can to make a distinctive contribution to a Christ-glorifying, earth-shaking revival of God's people in my generation.
199. I will build relationships that will help me and us to accomplish the call of God on our lives.
200. I will team up with the saints for God's greatest glory.
201. I will see an opportunity in every difficulty.

202. I will not wait for success to come to me. I will go to success, wherever it is.
203. I will not pursue joy, I will create it.
204. I will labour to think God's thoughts in every situation.
205. I will labour to speak God's language in every situation.
206. I will labour to carry out God's deeds in each situation.
207. I commit myself never to be idle.
208. I make the Lord Jesus the Healer of my body.
209. I will give God all the glory for each success of my life and each success of our ministry.
210. I will promote people.
211. I will start and finish each God-given project.
212. I will keep every command that the Lord has ever given me.
213. I will execute every commitment that I have ever made to the Lord.
214. I will fear the Lord.
215. I will be a man of integrity.
216. I will put in my all to be a model.
217. I will not seek to succeed alone.
218. I will share the vision.
219. I will seek, find, and incorporate co-workers into the vision.
220. I will put my all into anything I do.
221. I will live every day as if it were my last day on earth.
222. I will invest every hour as if it were the very last before I appear before the Judgment Seat of Christ.
223. We will make a distinct contribution to God's purposes in our generation by recruiting, training, sending, funding and upholding 10.000 national missionaries for church planting in all the nations of the world.

224. We will make a distinct contribution to God's purposes in our generation by selecting, training, sending, funding and upholding 10.000 international missionary couples for church planting in 200 nations of the Planet Earth.

225. We will invest all that we are and all that we have into the vision in order to accomplish the goal , yet we will depend solely on the Holy Spirit and His power for each and for all success.

226. I will spend every day on earth in eager and constant expectation of the return of my heavenly Lover (the Lord Jesus-Christ) and by what I am, by what I have and by what I do, hasten His return.

CHAPTER 17

THE BATTLE TO GIVE GOD A PROPHET FOR ISRAEL : HANNAH'S IMPORTUNITY

HANNAH KEPT ON PRAYING TO THE LORD

There are many reasons why people do not receive what they ask of God in prayer. One of the main reasons why most people do not receive what they ask of God in prayer is that they give up asking before they have prayed through.

You may ask, " What does it mean to pray through ? " To pray through is to pray and keep on praying until there is an assurance from the Lord that you have been heard and the answer granted. So to pray through the praying person keeps on praying to the Lord. To keep on praying to the Lord is to importune the Lord. It will be good for us to look at some examples of people who kept on importuning in prayer.

THE IMPORTUNITY OF THE FRIEND AT MIDNIGHT

The Bible says, " *Then he said to them, 'Suppose one of you has a friend, and he goes to him at midnight and says, 'Friend, lend me three loaves of bread, because a friend of mine on a journey has come to me, and I have nothing to set before him.' Then the one inside answers, ' Don't bother me. The door is already locked, and my children are with me in bed. I can't get up and give you anything.' I tell you, though he will not get up and give him the bread because he is his friend, yet because of the man's persistence he will get up and give him as much as he needs. So I say to you : Ask and it will be given to you ; seek and you will find ; knock and the door will be opened to you. For everyone who asks receives ; he who seeks finds ; and to him who knocks, the door will be opened* " (Luke 11 :5-10).

The friend at midnight importuned. The initial reply that he received was : " Don't bother me. I can't get up and give you anything. " However, because he persisted the friend got up and gave him not just anything but as much as he needed. Persistence enabled a person to move from the possibility of receiving nothing to the certainty of having as much as he needed.

There are three levels of importunity. We can set them forth as follows :

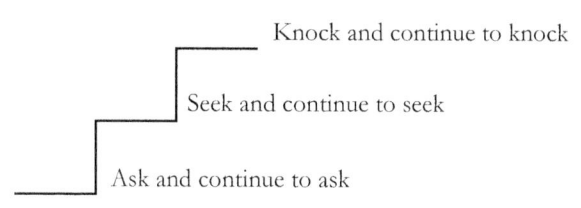

```
            ┌──── Knock and continue to knock
       ┌────┘ Seek and continue to seek
  ─────┘ Ask and continue to ask
```

There is, first of all, asking. This is continued until there is sustained asking. If the required answer is not received, the praying person moves to the plane of seeking for an answer. The seeking is started and continued persistently. This goes on and on until all the seeking has been carried out. If the desired result is still not obtained, the praying person moves to the plane of knocking. He knocks and continues knocking. He knocks with an increasing number of knocks per unit time. He may knock initially at the rate of three knocks per minute. Then he moves on to four, five, six, seven, eight, nine and ten knocks a minute. So the number of knocks increases directly with increasing time. We can represent this as follows :

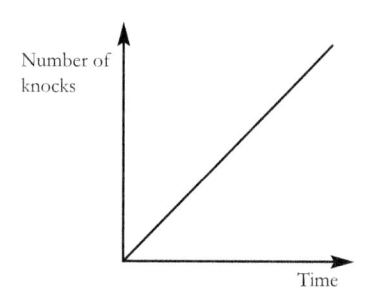

[Graph: Number of knocks (y-axis) vs Time (x-axis), showing a straight line increasing from origin]

The praying person does not only increase the number of knocks. He increases the intensity of knocking - each knock is more and more violent in such a way that the violence is directly proportional to time. We can represent this as follows:

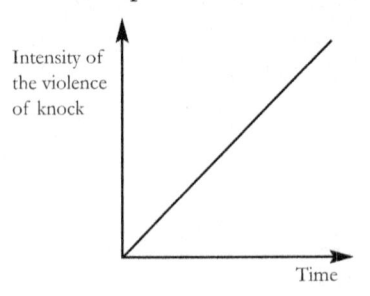

[Graph: Intensity of the violence of knock vs. Time, showing a linear increase]

Before the time that the maximum frequency of knocking and the maximum intensity of knocking is reached, the Lord will have answered.

IMPORTUNITY A REQUIREMENT OF GOD THE FATHER

The Lord God Almighty said, " *I have posted watchmen on your walls, O Jerusalem ; they will never be silent day or night. You who call on the Lord, give yourselves no rest, and give him no rest till he establishes Jerusalem and makes her the praise of the earth* " (Isaiah 62 :6-7).

These watchmen were to give themselves no rest night and day. They were also to give God no rest night and day until God acted.

The Lord rebuked Israel's watchmen, saying, " *Israel's watchmen are blind, they all lack knowledge ; they are all mute dogs, they cannot bark ; they lie around and dream , they love to sleep* " (Isaiah 56 :10).

The Lord Almighty rebuked Israel, saying, " *Yet you have not called upon me, O Jacob, you have not wearied yourselves for me, O Israel* " (Isaiah 43 :22).

In importunity a praying person wearies himself for the Lord and keeps wearying himself in prayer until the answer comes.

IMPORTUNITY A REQUIREMENT OF THE LORD JESUS

The Bible says, " *Then Jesus told his disciples a parable to show them that they should always pray and not give up. He said : ' In a certain town there was a judge who neither feared God nor cared about men. And there was a widow in that town who kept coming to him with the plea, ' Grant me justice against my adversary.'*

For some time he refused. But finally he said to himself, ' Even though I don't fear God or care about men, yet because this widow keeps bothering me, I will see that she gets justice, so that she won't eventually wear me out with her coming !'

And the Lord said, Listen to what the unjust judge says. And will not God bring about justice for his chosen ones, who cry out to him day and night ? Will he keep putting them off ? I tell you, he will see that they get justice, and quickly. However, when the Son of Man comes, will he find faith on the earth ? ' " (Luke 18 :1-8).

Importunity is praying without giving up ! Importunity is praying with such persistence that it looks as if God were being bothered. Importunity is praying with such persistence that it appears as if man were wearing God out

Hannah kept on praying to the Lord ! Amen.

You too keep on praying to the Lord !

I too will keep on praying to the Lord !

CHAPTER 18

THE BATTLE TO GIVE GOD A PROPHET FOR ISRAEL : HANNAH PRAYING IN THE HEART

HANNAH PRAYING IN THE HEART

The Bible says, "*As she kept on praying to the Lord, Eli observed her mouth. Hannah was praying in her heart, and her lips were moving but her voice was not heard*" (1 Samuel 1:12-13).

Hannah was praying in her heart. What does this mean? We know that man is tripartite. He is

- blood
- muscles
- bones

} body

- emotion
- mind
- will

} soul

- communion
- intuition
- conscience

} heart (spirit)

We could present the above as follows:

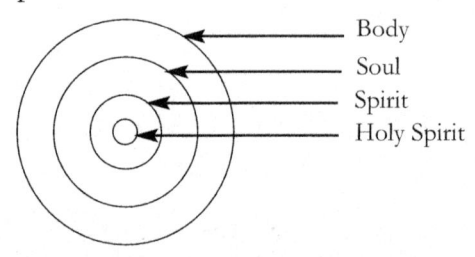

- Body
- Soul
- Spirit
- Holy Spirit

The Holy Spirit dwells in the spirit (heart) of the believer.

There could be prayer that has its origin in the human soul (mind) and is prayed to God. Such prayers are the ideas of man and they are vocalized (prayed with the voice, heard). There could also be prayer that has its origin in the Holy Spirit. The Holy Spirit initiates such praying, communicates it to the human spirit which then communicates it to the soul and then to the mouth where it is vocalized.

There is another type of prayer. In this type of praying, the Holy Spirit communicates God's burden to the human spirit. The human spirit picks this up and prays it back without words to the Holy Spirit and then sends information to the mind and from mind to the body where the mouth prays this aloud or silently.

In this case of Hannah's, the burden of the Lord was laid upon her human spirit by the Holy Spirit. She maintained communion between the human spirit and the Holy Spirit. It is as if the prayer originated with the Holy Spirit who laid the prayer burden on the human spirit, who in turn laid it on the Holy Spirit.

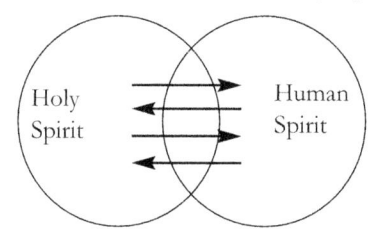

This goes on and on until the full burden that was on the Heart of the Holy Spirit has been deposited on the human spirit. The return to the Holy Spirit of all that He the Holy Spirit first laid on the human spirit signifies that the praying has ended. In the course of this praying in the heart, information is sent to the mouth by the mind. The mouth can pray what it has received aloud or silently. The mind could also keep the information without communicating it to the mouth.

PRAYING WITH THE HEART

When prayer is with the heart, the communication is predominantly or exclusively between the Holy Spirit and the human spirit. Such praying demands a pure heart for continuation. If there is sin in the heart, it will be impossible to have sustained communion between the human heart and the Holy Spirit. Those who carry unconfessed sin in their heart may occasionally have contact between the Holy Spirit and their human spirit, but sustained communion is excluded. Sustained praying with the heart is the privilege of those who will pay the price of walking in purity.

Why did Hannah communicate her praying to the mouth so that her lips were moving but her voice was not heard ? There are a number of possible reasons for this. The first one is that very few people are able to sustain prayer for long without the lips aiding the spirit. Most believers need the moving of lips to aid concentration in communion between the Holy Spirit and their spirit. Hannah might have needed this. The second reason is that the Holy Spirit moved her to pray in her heart with moving lips so that when it was time to be heard, the High Priest would speak to her.

We recommend that praying believers should actually learn, practise and master the spiritual art of praying with the heart without any sound being made with the lips. There is a certain point that can be reached in prayer where words become a distraction. There is praying with words known. There is also praying with words unknown. Thirdly, there is praying with moving lips but voice unheard. Fourthly, there is praying with groans. Lastly, there is praying without words. We can present these five forms of prayer as follows :

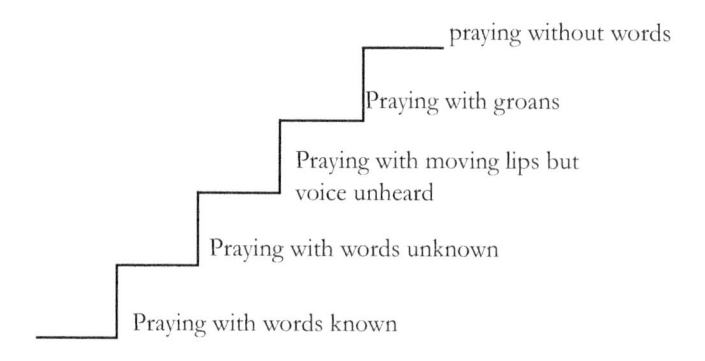

```
                                    ─── praying without words
                               ┌────┘
                               │ Praying with groans
                          ┌────┘
                          │ Praying with moving lips but
                          │ voice unheard
                     ┌────┘
                     │ Praying with words unknown
              ┌──────┘
       ───────┘ Praying with words known
```

The special point about praying without words is that purity of heart and intimacy with God at a much higher level are indispensable for this kind of praying. Those who pray at this plane pray out of union with God.

CHAPTER 19

THE BATTLE TO GIVE GOD A PROPHET FOR ISRAEL: HANNAH MISUNDERSTOOD

HANNAH MISUNDERSTOOD

" As she kept on praying to the Lord, Eli observed her mouth. Hannah was praying in her heart, and her lips were moving but her voice was not heard. Eli thought she was drunk and said to her, 'How long will you keep on getting drunk ? Get rid of your wine '" (1 Samuel 1 :12-14).

Hannah was caught up in very intense praying to God. She was praying in the heart and her lips were moving but her voice was not heard . She was in communion with God. Eli was the High Priest. He represented the highest level of human spiritual leadership. He, of all people, ought to have discerned immediately that she was praying. Unfortunately, he did not. Was it his physical sight that was growing dim and therefore prevented him from seeing well ? Was it because, having lost intimacy with God, he also lost the power for spiritual discernment ? Was it that many women often went to the temple and acted like drunkards so that he thought Hannah was acting like one of them ? We do not know what caused him to mistake her for a woman filled with wine but, all the same, he did and he spoke out.

ELI WAS NOT ALONE

Eli was not the only one who ever mistook people who were lost in prayer to God for drunkards. On the day of Pentecost when the one hundred and twenty were filled with the Holy Spirit and began to speak in other tongues as the Holy Spirit gave them utterance, some of those who heard them were amazed and perplexed while others said, *" They have had too much wine"* (Acts 2 :13).

YOU MAY BE MISUNDERSTOOD

If you make progress in the prayer life, if you separate yourself increasingly from people in order to pray, if you increasingly bear the Lord's burden and yoke, if you separate yourself increasingly from those things that will not advance the prayer life, if you devote more and more time to seek the Lord so as to know Him and, as a result of knowing Him, pray better, you will make progress in knowing the Lord and in praying to Him. However, some may misunderstand you and consider you weird, unbalanced, fanatical or as exaggerating.

If you are misunderstood, I encourage you to go on growing in the prayer life ; for the Lord Jesus understands.

Is it not enough that He understands ?

CHAPTER 20

THE BATTLE TO GIVE GOD A PROPHET FOR ISRAEL : HANNAH'S TRAVAILING THROUGH TO VICTORY

HANNAH'S TRAVAILING THROUGH TO VICTORY

"When speaking of compassion we briefly mentioned that type of prayer which includes a deep brokenness, sometimes even manifesting itself in groans. Such prayer would come under the category of " travail. " What exactly is travail ? Three basic facts about travail should provide an answer.

Travail is the dying part of prayer. An expectant mother often feels she is at the very brink of death during childbirth. The pain is such that even modern medication may fail to relieve all of it and the " labour " is actually very hard work. This pain is necessary and might be labelled the " *dying part* " of a mother's experience. Only as she willingly suffers and works can new life come forth " (Baker)

" *Before she goes into labour, she gives birth ;*
before the pains come upon her, she delivers a son.
Who has ever heard of such a thing ?
Who has ever seen such things ?
Can a country be born in a day
or a nation be brought forth in a moment ?
<u>*Yet no sooner is Zion in labour*</u>
<u>*than she gives birth to her children*</u>" (Isaiah 66 :7-8).

Travail comes through as the might, force, intensity of praying. The rate at which a delivery process advances and soon comes to an end is directly proportional to the might, force and intensity of the travail. We can present it as follows :

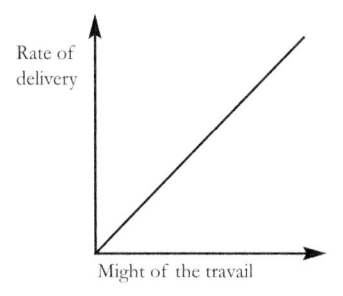

```
        Rate of
        delivery │        ╱
                 │       ╱
                 │      ╱
                 │     ╱
                 │    ╱
                 │   ╱
                 │  ╱
                 │ ╱
                 └─────────────▶
                  Might of the travail
```

The one who labours with great might will soon have what he labours for. The one who labours with little might will take much longer and may never be able to have the desired result. To ensure that the object desired in prayer is obtained a person should travail in total might. The same applies to the force and intensity. Maximum force and maximum intensity produce maximum results in minimum time.

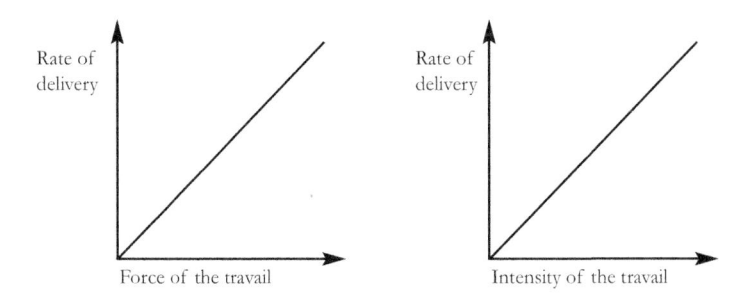

```
  Rate of                          Rate of
  delivery │      ╱                delivery │      ╱
           │     ╱                          │     ╱
           │    ╱                           │    ╱
           │   ╱                            │   ╱
           │  ╱                             │  ╱
           │ ╱                              │ ╱
           └──────────▶                     └──────────▶
            Force of the travail             Intensity of the travail
```

The force and intensity with which one prays cannot be made up. It is the outflow of the burden, the outflow of what would go wrong if God did not answer.

Hannah did not need to learn to pray with force, might and intensity. She was desperate to see the nation have a prophet; she was desperate to see a new day for the Israelites; she was desperate to see an end to her barrenness ; she was desperate to put an end to the provocations of Peninnah. The result of these things were that she flowed forth with deep longing and deep burning in prayer.

She said to Eli the High Priest, "*I am a woman who is deeply troubled. I have not been drinking wine or beer ; I was pouring out my soul to the Lord. Do not take your servant for a wicked woman ; I have been praying here out of my great anguish and grief*" (1 Samuel 1 :15-16).

We can say that the need in her heart led to deep pain and the deep pain led to great desire and the great desire led to fierce travail and the fierce travail gave way to great success.

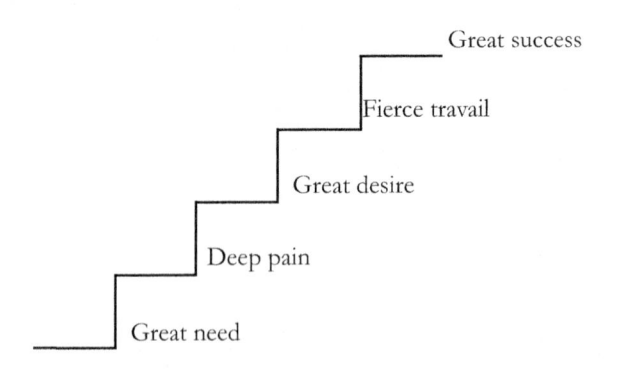

```
                                    ____ Great success
                               ____|
                              | Fierce travail
                        _____|
                       | Great desire
                  ____|
                 | Deep pain
            ____|
           | Great need
```

Because of Hannah's great need, deep pain and great desire, she could not help flowing out in ever increasing travail.

We can represent her travail, her labour pains, her putting all to have the " baby " born, her intense longing for fulfilment in the following way :

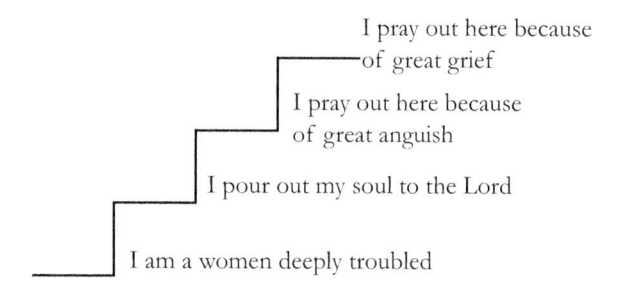

```
                              I pray out here because
                    ┌─────── of great grief
                    │         I pray out here because
              ┌─────┤         of great anguish
              │     I pour out my soul to the Lord
              │
       ───────┤  I am a women deeply troubled
```

She was deeply troubled. She reacted to this by pouring out her soul to the Lord. She continued to pray out of great anguish and continued to pray out of great grief. She got to the farthest place in supplication that she was able to reach. She got to her maximum limit and, because she had reached her maximum limit, God stepped in and answered her.

God will step in with answers and help from above when we have come to the end of ourselves, when we have invested our all. He will let us continue to struggle until we have come to the end of ourselves, until we have invested our all.

Could that be the reason why He has not yet answered you ? Could it be because there is a price to pay in supplication that you have not yet paid ? When a person gets to the place in his walk with God where his prayers flow from a life whose all has been laid on the altar of sacrifice for the Lord and for the Gospel , God answers his prayers most speedily.

Hannah had reached that place and it was only normal that God should step in at once. He stepped in.

PRAYER AND SPIRITUAL GROWTH

Hannah had grown in the course of praying. She went from weeping to much weeping. She went from bitterness of soul through great anguish to great grief. She went from praying to pouring out her soul to the Lord. She went from a woman who had no child to a woman who wanted a child and, finally, to a woman who wanted a child for the Lord.

Prayer is the place of growth in practically every domain of the spiritual life. The more a person prays the more he will know the Lord and, as he continues to pray, the more he will be transformed to be like the Lord to whom he is praying.

God gives Himself more to those of His children who invest more time in His presence waiting and praying to Him. How else could it be ?

CHAPTER 21

THE BATTLE TO GIVE GOD A PROPHET FOR ISRAEL : HANNAH'S SUPPLICATION AND FAITH

FAITH AND ANSWERS TO PRAYER

The Lord Jesus taught, saying, " *Therefore I tell you, whatever you ask for in prayer, believe that you have received it, and it will be yours* " (Mark 11:24).

James said, " *If any of you lacks wisdom, he should ask God, who gives generously to all without finding fault, and it will be given to him. But when he asks, he must believe and not doubt, because he who doubts is like a wave of the sea, blown and tossed by the wind. That man should not think he will receive anything from the Lord; he is a double-minded man, unstable in all he does* " (James 1:5-8).

There are three stages in asking and receiving things from God. These three stages are:

1. The stage of asking.
2. The stage of believing that what is asked for has been received.
3. The stage of seeing what has been received.

We have dealt extensively with the asking of Hannah in the parts of the book already treated. We must now concentrate on the receiving of what has been asked for.

It is man's duty to ask.
It is God's duty to give.
It is man's duty to receive what God has given.

If a person asks but is not able to receive what God gives, then he will not have what God has given.

WHAT GOD GIVES

God is Spirit. When He gives anything, He first gives it in the spirit form. The spirit form of anything is not visible to the physical eye, but it is visible to the spiritual eye. The spiritual eye is the eye of faith. The person who has faith receives what God has given in the invisible spirit form. He receives it in the invisible form and it is very real to him. He has seen it with the eye of faith, touched it with the hands of faith and embraced it with the bosom of faith.

What is received by faith, what is received in the invisible form, is later received in the physical, visible form.

The Lord Jesus demands that when someone asks something of Him, he should by faith receive it in the invisible form and afterwards what he received in the invisible form will be seen in the visible.

The promise of God to give you a thing makes the thing become immediately available in the spiritual (invisible) form. It should be received at once in that form and the Lord given thanks for having given. The one who has received what has been given manifests the fact that he has already received it in the invisible form (that is received it by faith) by never again asking for it but instead thanking God for having given what was asked. The time between receiving by faith and receiving by sight, which is also the time between receiving it in the invisible form and receiving it in the visible form, is to be filled with thanksgiving.

We can summarize this as follows :

1. Man asks of God.
2. God gives what has been asked for in the spirit form, which is the invisible form.
3. Man receives what God has given in the invisible form i.e. he receives it by faith.
4. Because man has already received what has been given by faith, he stops asking and begins to thank God for what has already been received by faith.
5. What was received by faith becomes visible.
6. Man continues to thank the Lord for what he received first by faith in the spirit form (invisible form) that has now become sight in the physical (visible form).

HANNAH AND THE RECEIVING OF SAMUEL

The Bible says, " *As she kept on praying to the Lord, Eli observed her mouth. Hannah was praying in her heart, and her lips were moving but her voice was not heard. Eli thought she was drunk and said to her, 'How long will you keep on getting drunk ? Get rid of your wine.'*

' Not so my Lord,' Hannah replied. ' I am a woman who is deeply troubled. I have not been drinking wine or beer. I was pouring out my soul to the Lord. Do not take your servant for a wicked woman ; I have been praying here out of my great anguish and grief.'

Eli answered, ' Go in peace, and may the God of Israel grant you what you have asked of him.'

She said, ' May your servant find favour in your eyes.' Then she went her way and ate something, and her face was no longer downcast. Early the next morning they arose and worshipped before the Lord and then went back to their home at Ramah. Elkanah lay with Hannah his wife, and the Lord remembered her. So in the course of time Hannah conceived and gave birth to a son. She named him Samuel, saying, 'Because I asked the Lord for him '" (1 Samuel 1:12-20).

First of all, Hannah prayed through. She got to a point in her asking God for a son where she could go no further. There was nothing she could do to plead with God that she did not do. She poured out her soul to the Lord out of her great anguish and out of her great grief! There was nothing that she held back from God. There was nothing that she spared herself of. She had put in everything. She reached the point where she touched God with her request.

Secondly, Eli brought her God's word. Eli said, "*Go in peace, and may the God of Israel grant you what you have asked of him*" (1 Samuel 1:17). What Eli said could be rephrased as follows, "Go in peace. The God of Israel has granted you what you have asked of him."

Thirdly, Hannah received what God offered through Eli. She said, "May your servant find favour in your eyes." What Hannah said could be rephrased as follows, "Your servant has found favour in your eyes." Or, it could be rephrased, "Your servant has found favour in the eyes of the God of Israel."

So Hannah had asked for a son.

God gave her the son through the words of the High Priest Eli

She received the son from God by believing what Eli said.

We can illustrate it as follows :

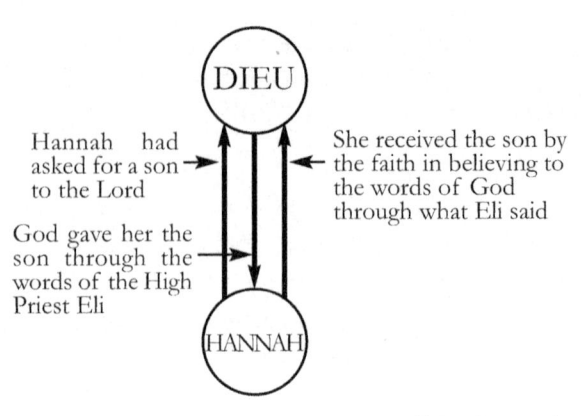

```
                    DIEU
Hannah had          ↑  ↑       She received the son by
asked for a son →   |  |  ←    the faith in believing to
to the Lord         |  |       the words of God
                    |  |       through what Eli said
God gave her the    |  |
son through the  ───┤  |
words of the High   |  |
Priest Eli          ↓  |
                   HANNAH
```

God gave Hannah the son in the invisible form through the words of the High Priest. He said, " Go in peace, the God of Israel has granted you what you asked of him . "

Hannah received the son in the invisible form (by faith) as she responded to the words of the High Priest of God, saying, " Your servant has found favour in your eyes. "

FAITH IS NOW

Faith is now : " The God of Israel has granted you what you asked of him. " Faith is now : " Your servant has found favour in your eyes. " We can illustrate it as follows :

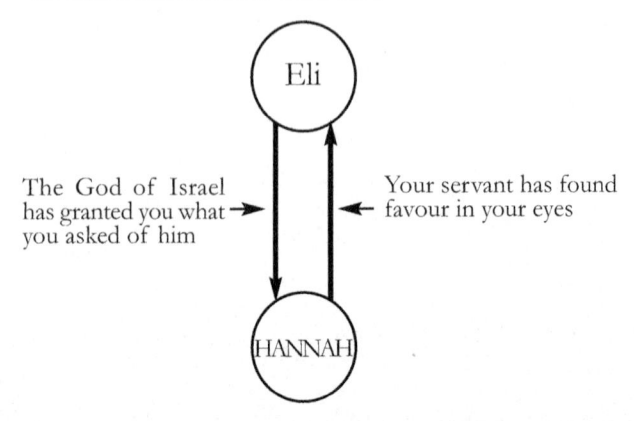

```
                     Eli
The God of Israel    ↑ ↑      Your servant has found
has granted you what→| |  ←   favour in your eyes
you asked of him     | |
                     ↓ |
                    HANNAH
```

Faith is now ! The Bible says, " *Faith is being sure of what we hope for and certain of what we do not see"* (Hebrews 11:1). Faith is being certain of what we do not see with the visible eye, but we have already seen in the invisible form with the eye of faith.

By faith Noah, when warned about things not yet seen (with physical eyes but seen with the eyes of the spirit) in holy fear built an ark to save his family. For the one hundred years that it took Noah to build the ark, the ark and the flood were already there before him in the spirit from the very moment when God spoke. He was walking by faith which means that he was walking by what he saw with spiritual eyes. We can illustrate what happened to Noah as follows :

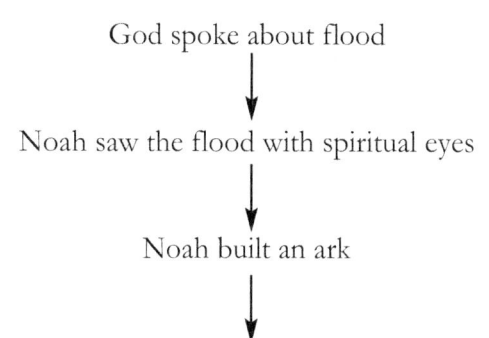

God spoke about flood
↓
Noah saw the flood with spiritual eyes
↓
Noah built an ark
↓
When ark was built Noah saw the flood with physical eyes

Faith without works is dead !

When a person says that he has seen with spiritual eyes (which is the same as saying that he has faith), he will act. If there are no acts, then the person has not seen with spiritual eyes. He has no faith.

Noah saw with spiritual eyes and acted. His acts proved that he saw. His acts, long before the flood became visible, one hundred years before the flood became visible, attest to his faith.

THE FAITH OF HANNAH

Hannah believed the Lord. Hannah believed what the High Priest said . Hannah received a son in the invisible form. Hannah received a son in the spirit. What proof is there about her faith ? The proof is in the acts that followed :

1. She went her way and ate something. She stopped her fast. The purpose of the fast was to move God to act in her favour. God had acted and there was no longer any reason for the fast.

2. Her face was no longer downcast. Her face had been downcast because she was barren. Now she was no longer barren. She had received a son by faith from the Lord. She had seen and received a son in her spirit, and that son was truly real to her. Because her barrenness was over, her being downcast was also over.

3. She and her husband returned to their home. They had received the desired son.

FAITH AND THE POINT OF CONTACT

Sometimes points of contact help people to release their faith. Hannah had laboured and laboured in asking the Lord to give her a son. When the High Priest Eli spoke, his word gave her a point of contact, and her faith was released. We can illustrate it as follows :

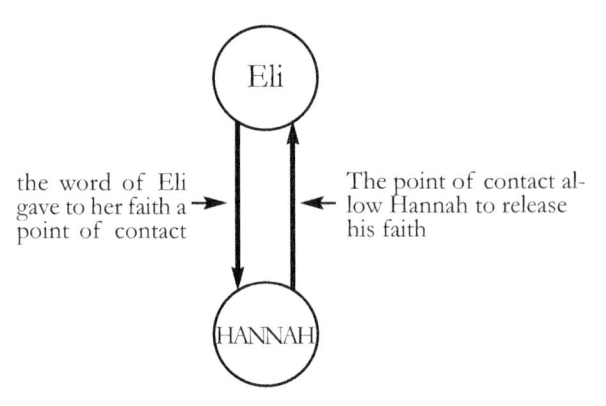

```
                    ┌─────┐
                    │ Eli │
                    └─────┘
the word of Eli        ↓↑          The point of contact al-
gave to her faith a  →    ←        low Hannah to release
point of contact                   his faith
                   ┌───────┐
                   │HANNAH │
                   └───────┘
```

We have found that during the ministry of the baptism of the Holy Spirit, the laying on of hands often provides the point of contact so that the person can release his faith and begin to praise God in a heavenly language.

We have also often found that many people are not able to receive their healing until hands are laid on them or until they are anointed with oil for healing in the Lord's name. When they are anointed or hands are laid upon them, their faith is released and they immediately enter into their inheritance. It is obvious that there is no power per se in the oil with which a person is anointed. We also know that there is no power in the human hands that are laid on a person. We, however, know that the oil or the hands provide a point of contact that enables a person to release his faith and receive what the Lord has given him.

The Lord Jesus used different points of contact as He ministered to people. Let us look at a few of them :

1. *"On a Sabbath Jesus was teaching in one of the synagogues, and a woman was there who had been crippled by a spirit for eighteen years. She was bent over and could not straighten up at all. When Jesus saw her, he called her forward and said to her, ' Woman, you are set free*

from your infirmity. *Then he put his hands on her, and immediately she straightened up and praised God*" (Luke 13:10-13). The Lord proclaimed her healed but went ahead to put His hands on her. When He laid hands on her she immediately straightened up and praised God! The laying of His hands on her provided the point of contact for her faith to be released; so that she could enter into the healing that was offered her when our Lord proclaimed her free.

2. "*As Jesus was on his way, the crowds almost crushed him. And a woman was there who had been subject to bleeding for twelve years, but no-one could heal her. She came up behind him and touched the edge of his cloak, and immediately her bleeding stopped. 'Who touched me?' Jesus asked. When they all denied it, Peter said, 'Master, the people are crowding and pressing against you.* *But Jesus said, ' Someone touched me; I know that power has gone out from me.* *Then the woman, seeing that she could not go unnoticed, came trembling and fell at his feet. In the presence of all the people, she told why she had touched him and how she had been instantly healed. Then he said to her, 'Daughter, your faith has healed you. Go in peace '*" (Luke 8:42b-48). Indeed her faith healed her, but she needed the contact with the cloak of the Lord Jesus for her faith to be released. Praise the Lord!

FROM FAITH TO SIGHT

We have seen that what God gives is first received by faith and this is receiving it in the invisible form. It is receiving it in the spirit form. When it is received by faith, faith carries out works so that it may not be dead faith. The works of faith may be a confession that proclaims that what is yet seen only with the eyes of faith has been received. The work of faith could also be thanksgiving.

Those who have faith confess what God has done before it becomes visible. They are not afraid to confess, because they have actually seen it and touched it in the invisible ! Often they thank the Lord for what they have received, which will become manifest in God's own time.

When a thing has been received by faith, we should not ask again. Asking again is unbelief and it nullifies what has been received. Confession and thanksgiving are the two things that are open to us.

There may be a lapse of time between the receiving by faith and the seeing with physical sight of what has been received by faith. That lapse of time is a matter of God's sovereignty, and we cannot do anything about it. We must stand on our faith and praise Him for what He has already done. The lapse of time between receiving by faith and seeing with physical sight could be

- one second,
- ten seconds,
- one minute,
- ten minutes,
- one hour,
- ten hours,
- one day,
- ten days,
- one week ,
- many weeks,
- one month,
- many months,
- one year,
- many years.

For Noah, it took one hundred years from the time when he saw the flood by faith till when he saw it physically. He needed those years to build the ark and get all the animals ready.

For Abraham, he waited for nearly twenty-five years before what he received by faith (a son) could become sight with the birth of Isaac. During those many years the Bible says, "*He is our father in the sight of God, in whom he believed the God who gives life to the dead and calls things that are not as though they were. Against all hope, Abraham in hope believed and so became the father of many nations, just as it had been said to him, 'So shall your offspring be.' Without weakening in his faith, he faced the fact that his body was as good as dead since he was about a hundred years old and that Sarah's womb was also dead. Yet he did not waver through unbelief regarding the promise of God, but was strengthened in his faith and gave glory to God, being fully persuaded that God had power to do what he had promised*" (Romans 4 :17-21).

We do not know how long Hannah had to wait. However, the Bible says, "*Early the next morning they arose and worshipped before the Lord and then went back to their home at Ramah. Elkanah lay with Hannah his wife, and the Lord remembered her. So in the course of time Hannah conceived and gave birth to a son. She named him Samuel, saying, 'Because I asked the Lord for him'*" (1 Samuel 1 :19-20).

God had kept His word !
Faith had become sight !

Glory be to God ! ! !

Samuel was alive. He was visible !
Amen.

CHAPTER 22

Consolidating The Gains From Supplication : Fulfilment Of The Vow

HANNAH FULFILLED HER VOW

THE VOW

Hannah had made a vow, saying, " *O Lord Almighty, if you will only look upon your servant's misery and remember me, and not forget your servant but give her a son, then I will give him to the Lord for all the days of his life, and no razor will ever be used on his head* " (1 Samuel 1 :11).

Hannah said that if God gave her a son, she would do the following :
1. Give him to the Lord for all the days of his life.
2. No razor would ever be used on his head.

In the first part of the vow, her son would never really be hers. He would belong to the Lord all the days of his life. In a sense, she was to derive no benefits from the boy. The Lord was to have him for Himself all the days of his life. The only joy that was to be hers was that of meeting the Lord's needs. So her son was to have a background of an entirely consecrated mother and would himself be entirely consecrated. We know that there is a relationship between the consecration of the parents and the consecration of the child. There is a sense in which the consecration of the child is directly proportional to the consecration of the parents. We can present this as follows :

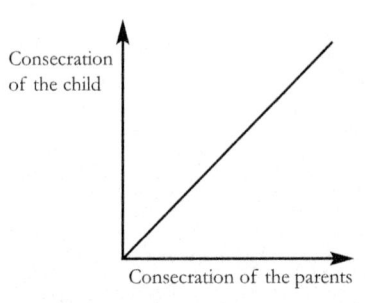

Hannah knew that if she separated herself from the boy, the boy would separate himself unto God. There is a sense in which there is a link between the extent to which a parent separates himself from his son and the extent to which the son separates himself unto God. Those parents who let their children go so that they might be all that God wants them to be, soon find that these children lay hold of God to a far-reaching extent. We can represent this by saying that the child's separation unto God is directly proportional to the parents' separation from the child.

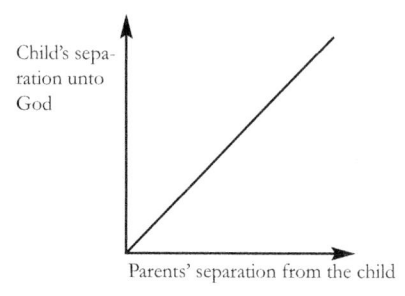

[Graph: Y-axis labeled "Child's separation unto God"; X-axis labeled "Parents' separation from the child"; showing a straight line rising from the origin.]

Those parents who do not allow their children the freedom to seek, know and do God's will for their lives but want to manipulate the children to become what they (the parents) want, will find that by their wrong influence the children are hindered from becoming all that God meant them to be.

Are you a parent ?

Have you completely abandoned your own desires, plans, schemes, etc, for your child ?

Are you praying that God's will and His will alone be done in your child's life ?

Have you ever prayed, saying, " My Lord, do Your will in my child and through my child at any cost to me " ?

If you have never prayed that way, will you pray that way now?

In the first part of the vow Hannah put a knife, first of all, into her own desires and, secondarily, into her son's desires. If God gave her a son, that son would never be hers to possess and keep. If God gave her a son, that son would never belong to himself. He would belong to another. He would belong to God. So the vow made mother and son losers.

In the second part of the vow, if God gave Hannah a son, no razor would ever be used on his head! Hannah was saying, " God, if you give me a son, that son will not conform to the appearance of the people around. He will be frightful, strange, unlike the others !" Hannah was setting her son apart. She was offering him, not the comfort of being like others, but the discomfort of being unlike others. Physically, her son would not be able to be like others. Being different was imposed on him by his mother's vow, by his mother's consecration.

The world calls for conformity. The Lord calls for transformation. The Bible says, " *Therefore, I urge you, brothers, in view of God's mercy, to offer your bodies as living sacrifices, holy and pleasing to God - this is your spiritual act of worship. Do not conform any longer to the pattern of this world, but be transformed by the renewing of your mind. Then you will be able to test and approve what God's will is - his good, pleasing and perfect will*" (Romans 12:1-2).

Closeness to God and usefulness in His service are directly proportional to the extent to which someone has separated himself from conformity to the world, and also directly proportional to the extent to which someone has allowed the Holy Spirit to transform him.

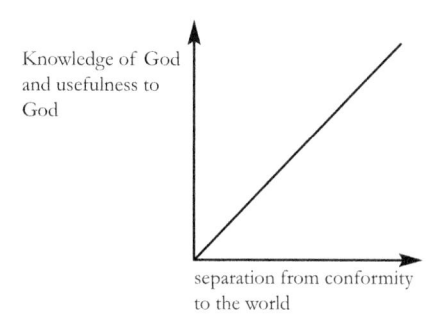

[Graph: y-axis "Knowledge of God and usefulness to God"; x-axis "separation from conformity to the world"; diagonal line showing direct proportionality]

The one who is not separated from conformity to the world will not know God and will not be useful to God. The one who separates himself completely from conformity to the world will know God much and be very useful to God. Similarly, usefulness to God is directly proportional to the extent to which the person has been transformed by the renewing of the mind.

[Graph: y-axis "Knowledge of God and usefulness to God"; x-axis "transformation by the renewing of the mind"; diagonal line showing direct proportionality]

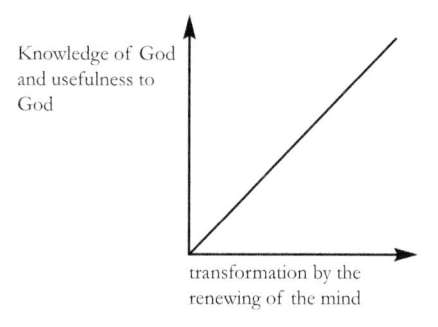

Those who are transformed, those who are separated from conformity to the world are strange. They appear to the worldly to be abnormal. The apostles were like that. The Apostle Paul wrote, *" For it seems to me that God has put us apostles on display at the end of the procession, like men condemned to die in the arena. We have been made a spectacle to the whole universe, to angels as well as to men. We are fools for Christ, but you are so wise in Christ ! We are weak, but you are strong ! You are honoured, we are dishonoured ! To this very hour we go hungry and thirsty, we are in rags, we are brutally treated, we are ho-*

meless. We work hard with our own hands. When we are cursed, we bless ; when we are persecuted, we endure it, when we are slandered, we answer kindly. Up to this moment we have become the scum of the earth, the refuse of the world" (1 Corinthians 4 : 9-13).

HANNAH KEPT HER VOW

The Bible says, *" So in the course of time Hannah conceived and gave birth to a son. She named him Samuel, saying, 'Because I asked the Lord for him.'*

When the man Elkanah went up with all his family to offer the annual sacrifice to the Lord and to fulfil his vow, Hannah did not go. She said to her husband, 'After the boy is weaned, I will take him and present him before the Lord, and he will live there always.'

'Do what seems best to you,' Elkanah her husband told her. 'Stay here until you have weaned him, only may the Lord make good his word.' So the woman stayed at home and nursed her son until she had weaned him.

After he was weaned, she took the boy with her, young as he was, along with a three-year-old bull, an ephah of flour and a skin of wine, and brought him to the house of the Lord at Shiloh. When they had slaughtered the bull, they brought the boy to Eli, and she said to him, 'As surely as you live, my lord, I am the woman who stood here beside you praying to the Lord. I prayed for this child, and the Lord has granted me what I asked of him. So now I give him to the Lord. For his whole life he shall be given over to the Lord '" (1 Samuel 1 :20-28).

<u>I believe that there is a relationship between integrity and answers to prayer</u>. Those who make promises to God and do not keep them are doubtful persons. How can God take them to heart ? Elkanah said, " Only may the Lord make good his word. " We say that the

Lord makes good His word to those who make good their word. To those who make promises but do not fulfil them, He has no obligation. The Bible says " *To the faithful you show yourself faithful, to the blameless you show yourself blameless, to the pure you show yourself pure, but to the crooked you show yourself shrewd* " (Psalm 18 :25-26).

To the crooked person who makes promises to God but does not keep them, God will not show Himself to him as faithful, blameless or pure. God will show Himself to that one as shrewd.

Those who fulfil their vows, keep their promises, walk in truth, have a claim on the Lord in prayer that those who are deceitful (by making promises that they do not keep) do not have. God goes out of His way to answer the petition of those of integrity. The hypocrite, liar, covenant-breaker often does not have inner courage to press through in prayer. He, consequently, cannot move God to answer !

We conclude that the extent to which the Lord will answer a person's prayer is directly proportional to that one's integrity. Those who are true to God and man and keep their word to God and man are God's favourites, and He answers them with favour. We present this truth as follows :

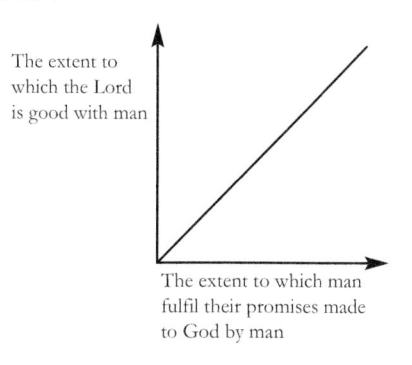

[Graph: Y-axis labeled "The extent to which the Lord is good with man"; X-axis labeled "The extent to which man fulfil their promises made to God by man"; showing a straight diagonal line rising from the origin.]

If you have outstanding unanswered prayers, it may be because you have outstanding vows, covenants, promises proclamations unfulfilled to God and man.

Hannah was different. She kept her vow.

You, too, be different. Keep your word.

I, too, will be different. I will keep my word.

Amen!

CHAPTER 23

Consolidating The Gains From Supplication : Hannah's Praise And Thanksgiving

HANNAH'S PRAISE AND THANKSGIVING

Then Hannah prayed and said :

" *My heart rejoices in the Lord ; in the Lord my horn is lifted high. My mouth boasts over my enemies , for I delight in your deliverance.*

There is no-one holy like the Lord ; there is no-one besides you ; there is no Rock like our God.

Do not keep talking so proudly or let your mouth speak such arrogance, for the Lord is a God who knows , and by him deeds are weighed.

The bows of the warriors are broken, but those who stumbled are armed with strength.

Those who were full hire themselves out for food, but those who were hungry hunger no more. She who was barren has borne seven children, but she who has had many sons pines away.

The Lord brings death and makes alive, he brings down to the grave and raises up. The Lord sends poverty and wealth ; he humbles and he exalts. He raises the poor from the dust and lifts the needy from the ash heap ; he seats them with princes and has them inherit a throne of honour.

For the foundations of the earth are the Lord's ; upon them he has set the world. He will guard the feet of his saints, but the wicked will be silenced in darkness.

It is not by strength that one prevails ; those who oppose the Lord will be shattered. He will thunder against them from heaven ; the Lord will judge the ends of the earth.

He will give strength to his king and exalt the horn of his anointed "

(1 Samuel 2:1-10).

HANNAH'S PRAISE

When the Lord reveals the greatness of His being; i.e. who He is, the person who receives the revelation responds with praise. In the case at hand, God's goodness in giving Hannah a son revealed His character. She said, " There is no-one holy like the Lord; there is no-one besides you; there is no Rock like our God. " She continued to praise the Lord, saying, " The Lord is a God who knows, and by him deeds are weighed . "

So praise exalts the Lord for whom He is. The Lord revealed His being to her and she responded with praise.

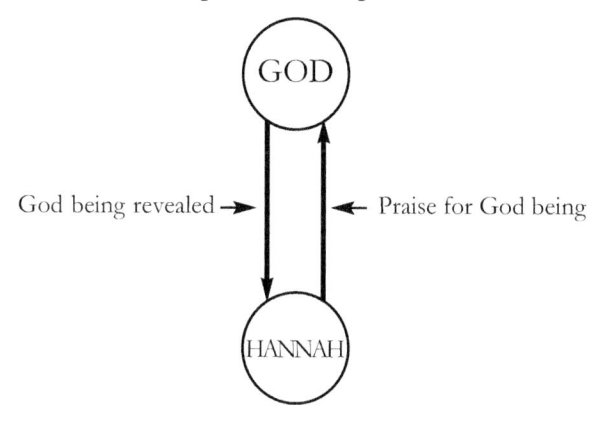

```
         GOD
          ↕
God being revealed →   ← Praise for God being
          ↕
        HANNAH
```

Hannah received a revelation of God's person and praised the Lord. We must each seek the Lord and receive a revelation of His person and respond with special praise. While we wait for that special revelation, let us begin to praise Him for what He has revealed of Himself in the Word.

The Psalmist proclaimed ;
" *Let them praise the name of the Lord,*
for his name alone is exalted ;
his splendour is above the earth and the heavens " (Psalm 148 :13-14).

Let us do the same.
Amen.

HANNAH'S THANKSGIVING

Thanksgiving is praising the Lord for His deeds- for what He did, for what He is doing and for what He will do. In the case at hand , the Lord gave Hannah a son. She did not hide her joy. Her joy and her praise were united, welded together. She said the following, "*My heart rejoices in the Lord, in the Lord my horn is lifted high. My mouth boasts over my enemies, for I delight in your deliverance. The bows of the warriors are broken, but those who stumbled are armed with strength. She who was barren has borne seven children. He raises the poor from the dust and lifts the needy from the ash heap ; he seats them with princes and has them inherit a throne of honour. It is not by strength that one prevails ; those who oppose the Lord will be shattered. He will thunder against them from heaven ; the Lord will judge the ends of the earth. He gives strength to the king and exalts the horn of his anointed*" (1 Samuel 2 : 1-10).

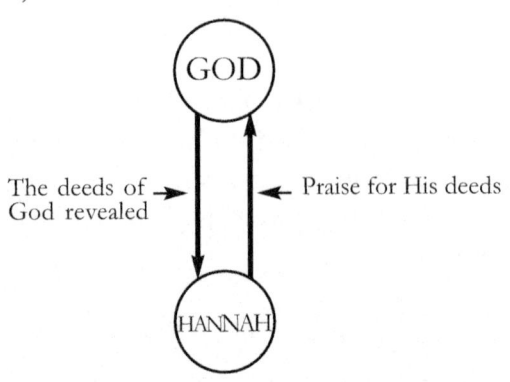

Hannah thanked the Lord for His deeds of the past and for His deed for her in giving her a son. Have you also thanked the Lord for His deeds for you ? Why don't you stop and write down 100 things that the Lord has done for you this year ? After writing them, will you thank the Lord for each one of them systematically ?

Do not take the Lord for granted. Do not ask things of Him and when He has given them to you, you fail to come back to Him in expression of gratitude. Ingratitude is a terrible sin. Do not commit it. Commit the righteousness of gratitude. Begin now !

Amen.

CHAPTER 24

In Conclusion :
A Praying Prophet

A PRAYING PROPHET

Samuel did become a prophet.

The Nation of Israel had a seer.

The nation had a praying prophet.

Samuel said to Israel, "*As for me, far be it fromm e that I should sin against the Lord by failing to pray for you*" (1 Samuel 12 :23).

A PRAYING PROPHET

Hannah was a woman of prayer. In fact, without violent prayer Samuel would never have been born. He must have received something of prayer in his spiritual genetic make-up. In addition, he was faced with circumstances that compelled prayer. So he became a praying prophet.

I WILL INTERCEDE FOR YOU

The Bible says, "*Then Samuel said, 'Assemble all Israel at Mizpah and I will intercede with the Lord for you*'" (1 Samuel 7 :5). Samuel walked with God. Israel was oppressed by the Philistines. Only God could deliver Israel. For God to deliver Israel, Samuel needed to intercede . He offered to intercede. They confessed their sin and put away all that was not pleasing to the Lord.

The Israelites said to Samuel, "*Do not stop crying out to the Lord our God for us, that he may rescue us from the hand of the Philistines*" (1 Samuel 7 :8). Samuel was a man who was able to cry out to the Lord so that He should do something. His mother cried out to the Lord that Samuel should be born. Now Samuel was being asked not to stop crying out to the Lord for the safety of Israel. The Israelites felt that the situation needed crying out. They also knew that Samuel was able to cry out to the Lord on their behalf. They also felt that he cared enough to be willing to cry out on their behalf.

Are you able to cry out?

Do you care enough about someone not just to pray for him but also to cry out to the Lord on his behalf? Who is that person?

Are you facing a situation in your ministry that demands crying out to the Lord?

Have you cried out?

THE CRYING PROPHET

The Israelites had demanded that Samuel should cry out to the Lord on their behalf. They had demanded that he cry out unceasingly. Samuel did cry out, but before crying out he made an offering to the Lord. The Bible says, "*Then Samuel took a suckling lamb and offered it up as a whole burnt offering to the Lord. He cried out to the Lord on Israel's behalf, and the Lord answered him*" (1 Samuel 7:9).

Samuel could have cried out to the Lord without offering the sacrifice and the Lord would still have heard him. However, like his mother who could have been heard even if she had not made a vow, yet she made a vow, he sacrificed to the Lord before he cried out to Him on behalf of Israel.

There are people who ask, "How can we get the maximum from God while giving Him the minimum? Such speak from a poor relationship with God. However, for those who love the Lord, for those who have matured in their relationship with God, the thought of holding back anything from God is non-existent. They love God and they want to give Him their all. They do not just want things from God, they want to please God. And God is glad with their attitude.

God does not give more to the one who sacrifices before crying out to Him than He gives to the one who cries out to Him without sacrificing anything. The difference lies in the fact that His lovers, who bring the offering as well as their request, are closer to His heart than those who only come to Him with their need. The difference is great.

In offering the burnt offering to the Lord before crying out to Him, Samuel sought to renew fellowship and intimacy and then to cry out to God from intimacy. We can illustrate this as follows :

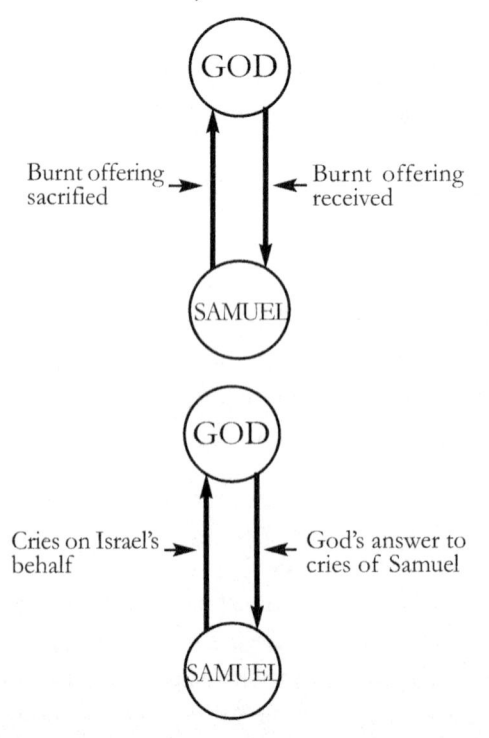

```
              ( GOD )
Burnt offering →   ← Burnt offering
sacrificed            received
              ↕
            (SAMUEL)


              ( GOD )
Cries on Israel's →   ← God's answer to
behalf                cries of Samuel
              ↕
            (SAMUEL)
```

Samuel cried out and he was heard. The crux of the matter is not just crying out to God. The crux of the matter lies in being heard by the Lord. Samuel knew God. He knew God's mind and he cried out in the centre of God's will and the Lord heard him.

Each one of us must build the type of relationship with God that will ensure that He hears us when we cry out to Him. Secondly, we must ensure that we are crying out to Him for things that are in the centre of His will. If we do that, we can be sure that He will hear us and give us our request.

Amen.

A MONUMENT-RAISING PROPHET

Many of God's children are tossed about by many doubts because they do not remember God's faithfulness of the past. The Psalmist cried out, " *Praise the Lord, O my soul, and forget not all his benefits* " (Psalms103 :2).

The children of Israel were forgetful to their own hurt. The Psalmist said, "*They did not remember his power the day he redeemed them from the oppressor, the day he displayed his miraculous signs in Egypt, his wonders in the region of Zoan* " (Psalm 78 :42-43).

The Prophet Samuel did not want to fall into such an error. He raised up a monument to remind him and all Israel about God's deliverance. The Bible says, " *Then Samuel took a stone and set it up between Mizpah and Shen. He named it Ebenezer, saying, ' Thus far has the Lord helped us* '" (1 Samuel 7 :12).

We can illustrate it as follows :

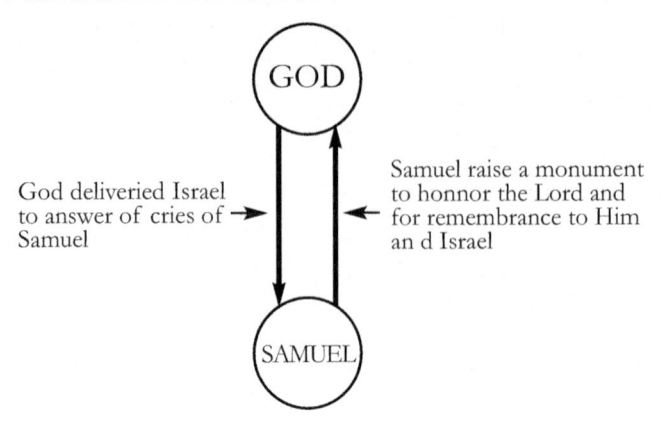

```
                    ┌─────┐
                    │ GOD │
                    └─────┘
                       ↕
God deliveried Israel →   ←  Samuel raise a monument
to answer of cries of        to honnor the Lord and
Samuel                       for remembrance to Him
                             an d Israel
                       ↕
                  ┌────────┐
                  │ SAMUEL │
                  └────────┘
```

When the Lord intervenes dramatically in your life, you should raise a monument of thanksgiving and of remembrance. Then the next time you face a difficulty you will confidently look up to Him, fully assured that just as He did not fail in the past, He will not fail in the future.

A PROPHET WHO WILL NOT COMMIT THE SIN OF PRAYERLESSNESS

The prophet Samuel said, " *As for me, far be it from me that I should sin against the Lord by failing to pray for you* " (1 Samuel 12 :23).

The prophet Samuel knew that prayerlessness was a sin. He knew that failure to pray for those he led was a sin.

Because he knew that prayerlessness was a sin, he determined not to commit that sin. His determination helped him to be faithful.

He was faithful.
He prayed.

Glory be to God !

I pray that you, too, like him, should not commit the sin of prayerlessness. You will not commit it because you pray and will keep on praying. Glory be to the Lord !

Printed in Great Britain
by Amazon